SITTING INSIDE

BUDDHIST PRACTICE IN AMERICA'S PRISONS

Kobai Scott Whitney

FOREWORD BY BO LOZOFF
EDITED BY KATE CRISP

PRISON DHARMA NEWORK
Boulder
2003

D1214953

PRISON DHARMA NETWORK
PO Box 4623
Boulder, CO 80306
www.PrisonDharmaNetwork.org

ISBN: 0-9718143-0-9

First Published June 2002
Second Edition March 2003

Distributed by Prison Dharma Network.

Cover Design by John Weber & Mary Sweet

Printed in the United States of America

DEDICATION

For Rob and Clyde and Calvin and Gunaratna

and Noah and Kent and Jarvis and Fleet

and for the unnamed inmates practicing.

For Robert and Robina and Joan and Deborah and Shugen

and

all the teachers, lamas, roshis—

and all the unnamed dharma volunteers.

And for the guards who endure great hardship too.

And for those we've caused to suffer.

All of us!

Everyday, trying to meet the moment.

May we all wake up together.

ACKNOWLEDGEMENTS

I would like to thank Parallax Press for their early support of this project, and Prison Dharma Network's Director Kate Crisp, who picked it up and ran with it.

My own sangha in Hawaii, Honolulu Diamond Sangha, and my fellow residents at Koko An Zendo have cheered me on and kept me going through every discouragement.

And I am grateful to Robert Aitken Roshi, my old teacher, who never retired enough not to help.

Many thanks to Bo Lozoff and Fleet Maull, whose contributions were invaluable.

Thank you to the prisoners and prison dharma volunteers who shared their insights and wisdom: Deborah Barrett, Arturo Esquel, Lama Yonton Gonpa, Kerry Greenwell, Joan Halifax, Mair Honan, John Daido Loori, Calvin Malone, Kobutsu Malone, Jarvis Masters, Lucia Meijer, Laine Moore, Kusala Ratnakarkuna, Gunaratna Sarika, Vivian Snyder, and Kent Wimberly.

Beverly Armstrong, proofreader, and John Weber, cover designer, generously donated their time, skills, and knowledge.

And special thanks to the Nalanda Individual Assistance Trust—in particular Pamela Krasney, Peter Goldfarb, Alex Halpern, Chris Hormel, Jeff Waltcher, and Thomas Hardy—whose generous support made publishing this book a reality.

Kobai Scott Whitney
Honolulu, Hawaii
January 1, 2002

CONTENTS

Tragic Necessities

We live in an era that will long be remembered for its shortsightedness and cruelty around issues of imprisonment. Especially in the United States—with the rest of the world typically following our lead—we seem to have descended into open madness when it comes to numbers of prisons, numbers of prisoners, architectural style of prisons and jails, life-without-parole sentences, treating younger and younger juveniles as adults, absence of rehabilitative programs and resources, and the overall mean-spiritedness that sets the policies and tone for daily life in most of our prisons. Political leaders across the entire spectrum from left to right, liberal to conservative, seem to find agreement in voicing harsh and misleading rhetoric about crime and its solutions. That rhetoric has resulted in the steepest rise of prison populations in history, housed in buildings that are so brutally anti-life that they defy all reason, logic and morality.

Nearly thirty years ago, my wife Sita and I took an interest in the spiritual possibilities for the men and women who find themselves incarcerated in this great beast. When we started the Prison-Ashram Project in 1973, most prisoners and prison officials had never heard of yoga, meditation, or Buddhism. That did not surprise us, but what did surprise us was the immediate and sincere interest among prisoners of every race and background. The project quickly became our life's work and continues to this day, with nearly half our staff now former prisoners who had benefited from their practice of these ideas and disciplines while they were locked up.

When we started our work, the entire U.S. prison population was around 185,000. Now, California has nearly that many, and so does Texas. In the year 2001, the United States held more than 25 percent of the world's prisoners, although we are but five percent of the world's population. Our Prison-Ashram Project is now, unfortunately, the world's largest interfaith prison ministry.

It is not a happy sight to see the problems getting worse and the country creating a curse on future generations by having so many cells to fill. Yet at the same time, it is heartening to watch the evolution of other faith-based groups doing prison work and touching many lives. As American Buddhism has found its ground and its path, "engaged Buddhism" has naturally found its way into the prison system. Many prisoners have been so turned off or turned away by their birth religions, that they are wide open to a system at once more practical and more spiritual (as opposed to religious), and so Buddhist thought and practice have made serious inroads into the bleakness of our penal institutions.

I know prisoners who use practices of *metta*, or loving-kindness, when thrown into solitary; others who practice *tonglen* for the benefit of prisoners and staff who seem to be enveloped in cruelty or brutality; others who use the Triple Refuge or Four Noble Truths to frame their lives in order to endure a death sentence or endless years of sitting in a small cell with nothing to do. The situation has become holocaustic. Prisoners' motivations have become urgent. And when motivation becomes urgent in the right way, the spiritual life opens like a flower.

Into this morass steps Kobai Scott Whitney, the new generation of spiritual prison activist who has personal experience of confinement and of the benefits of spiritual practice in confinement. Although his connection is specifically Buddhist, most of the book imparts views and practices that can help anyone of any faith in any situation. His Holiness the Dalai Lama has said time and time again that it is not important whether one becomes a Buddhist; it is important that we treat each other with kindness. In order to treat each other with kindness in the context of prison life, we must develop a great deal of insight, street-smarts, compassion, and discipline. Hence the ideas and practices in this book.

Western Buddhism is essentially in its second generation. Western Buddhism in prisons is in its first generation. I am certain it will continue to evolve from the experiences of both the teachers and their incarcerated students. Prison is currently a pretty terrible environment. Yet terrible environments can spur dramatic spiritual work and breakthroughs. One significant part of the evolution of Buddhism in prisons is finding the shifting balance between teachings and activism—sitting on the cushion and trying to change a monstrous system. I believe Scott Whitney touches clearly on both sides of that line in this volume. Without the inner work he describes, one's activism will likely lead to anger and frustration. Without any sociopolitical expression of our inner discoveries, one's meditation will likely become mere withdrawal and passivity.

Given the self-perpetuating loop of political rhetoric/media sensationalism/public ignorance, the truth about prisons, the truth about what works and what does not work to create a safer and more peaceful society, is not likely to become public knowledge anytime soon—especially since the advent of private profits as a motivation for building and filling prison cells. This book directly addresses the issue of empowering prisoners themselves, independent of external changes, however badly these are needed. A dysfunctional, violent prison system will tend to spit out dysfunctional, violent former prisoners. As of the year 2000, over 50,000 prisoners a year are being let out on the streets.

Our best hope for positive change lies, tragically, in the empowerment of individual prisoners to become deeper, more caring human beings *despite* the formidable odds against them. This is my hope for the present volume. My own prison work is wholly interfaith, so we will try to catch the prisoners who may not feel as inclined toward Buddhist terminology and views as expressed in Kobai's book. But anyone with an open mind and heart, whether or not she or he wishes to "become a Buddhist," will find many valuable insights and practices here for the cultivation of universal spiritual qualities that will help relieve suffering in any environment. We are truly all doing time, and all on the same journey. Understanding this is our best hope for the future.

Bo Lozoff

Holding Back Disaster

He who puts an end to former crimes
By taking up the way of peace,
Illuminates the world
Like the moon freed from a veil of clouds.

—*Angulimala Sutta*

Without much foresight, let alone wisdom, the United States has spent the last two decades imprisoning about two million of its adult citizens. We now lock up more of our population than does Russia, and more than any modern industrial democracy.

Despite the fact that U.S. crime rates have been decreasing since 1993, politicians play to the fears of the voters and strut in public to prove how tough they are on crime. New, more punitive sentencing laws have become popular with legislators and prosecutors and have resulted in an unprecedented increase in prison building. This boom in pork-barrel prison projects has taken up some of the slack created by the defense-spending cuts that followed the end of the cold war. Another war—the war on drugs—has led to the imprisonment of more than a million men and women, cutting them off from the treatment they need and the chance to change. Instead, we have given them a chance to deteriorate and to become less human.

Yet throughout this archipelago of razor-wired penal institutions, some inmates are making efforts to reform their behavior, values, thoughts, speech, and emotions. Many have begun looking to Buddhism as a way of making sense of their daily lives and as a way of coming to terms with the life-and-death issues of human life. Outside prison walls, American Buddhism is finding its own way within the religious and intellectual landscape of modern North America. Inmates have joined with others to explore alternatives to an unsatisfactory or nonexistent childhood experience with organized religion. American Buddhists have started responding to the inquiries and needs of prisoners who want to learn what Buddhism has to offer.

This book is written for these two audiences: inmates who want to start a Buddhist practice and Buddhists outside of prison who want to help them do so. Some chapters of this book, such as chapter 2, are intended especially for inmates; others, like chapter 6, are specifically for Buddhist prison volunteers.

I am writing for those who feel they are imprisoned as well as for those who think they are free. People in prisons are, of course, not physically free, but many have discovered their own liberation through meditation, the cultivation of compassion, and the practice of the Buddhist precepts. Prison guards think of themselves as free, because they live outside the perimeters of the prison walls and fences—yet many security workers are just as imprisoned as the inmates, trapped in a workplace of boredom, mistrust, and lurking violence. We who live outside sometimes feel unfree because we are imprisoned by our habits, fears, and impulses.

DOING TIME

My own prison experience was a decade ago, when I was given a six-month sentence for drug-related charges. I had been exposed to Buddhism many years before that, when I studied at Zen Center in San Francisco and, later, with Aitken Roshi at the Diamond Sangha in Honolulu. But my Zen was a kind of hobby. I liked the intellectual and aesthetic aspects of it. It was "trippy" and "cosmic," as we used to say in the 1970s. My practice was more involved with self-absorbed mind games than it was with compassion or ethical behavior. I continued to dabble in alcohol, drugs, and questionable sexual behavior. In the best of times,

I did *zazen,* the Japanese term for sitting meditation, about once a week. I now refer to those years as my *leisure* Zen period.

My time in prison became the turning point for my history as a Buddhist. All of a sudden it was imperative that I find out what had gone wrong. And, all of a sudden, I had the time to do this. In fact, I was "doing time."

Because of Buddhist practice, those six months in that sad place became a time of daily sitting meditation practice and attention to precepts—a time of simplicity and more happiness than I had known in years. Although (as in many prisons) alcohol and drugs were readily available, I stopped using all intoxicants. I was allowed to bring in my meditation cushion, called a *zafu* in Japanese, a Buddha image, and one book, a translation of writings by the thirteenth-century Zen master Dôgen.

Although my time in prison presented many difficulties and not a few dangers, I look back on that half year with a strange fondness. In addition to meditation and freedom from drugs and alcohol, I was also able to find useful tasks inside such as organizing the library and helping to start adult basic education classes. I enjoyed helping other inmates with their homework or with writing letters. As I look back, I see that the simple combination of daily meditation, freedom from addiction, and "prosocial," or useful, activities was a formula that helped me to prosper spiritually and emotionally during a time in my life that could have been filled with anger, anxiety, and bitterness. Years later, this three-part formula still keeps my life together.

My original subtitle for this book was "Buddhist Meditation in American Prisons." But I changed that subtitle to "Buddhist *Practice* in American Prisons." I did this to emphasize what I learned from my own experience—that dabbling in meditation is not sufficient to change a life. One of the first things I did when I returned home from prison was to go through a ceremony called *jukai* in the Zen tradition. This initiation meant that I was "officially" a Buddhist, with a Buddhist name, Kobai, which means "old plum" in Sino-Japanese. This ceremony is more universally called "taking refuge"—in the historical Buddha as a spiritually realized guide; in the *dharma,* his teaching; and in the *sangha,* the community of Buddhists. It is also in this ceremony that one "takes the precepts," which means one commits to ethical behavior. This commitment is what had been missing from my practice. The other important element I had been missing was a commitment to compassion as embodied in the *metta,* or "loving-kindness," teachings of the vipassana Buddhist tradition.

THE GREAT RECOVERY

Prisoners are often attracted to the idea of meditation. Sometimes, those who want to be Buddhists get obsessed with the exotica of Buddhism—incense containers, Buddha images, robes, and Buddhist rosaries. All these things are a small part of practice. But far more important is the extension of Buddhist behavior outside the meditation hall. This is what prison activist Bo Lozoff has referred to as "the Great Recovery." The formula for this recovery has three parts: regular practice of meditation, a commitment to ethical behavior, and the practice of open, accepting compassion for all our neighbors in this world.

I cannot describe from personal experience the feelings of inmates who live on death row, or who have been sentenced to life without the possibility of parole. Many of these prisoners live in hell-like institutions that authorities proudly call "supermaxes" or control units. In the pages of this book, you will hear from some of these long-term prisoners, who can speak eloquently and directly about the difficulties of practice in these "hell realms."

In the years since I was released, I have visited, spoken on the phone, and corresponded with prisoners around the country who have also discovered that "doing time" can become a fortunate opportunity to practice meditation. Some of these practitioners have become true scholars of Buddhism; others are more focused on time-tested contemplative practices from a variety of religious traditions, using these methods for stress reduction and to assist with character change. Some do not think of themselves as Buddhists. Yet Buddhism's simple program for a way to live has helped many inmates out of suffering and on toward the freedom that we all yearn for. At the core of Buddhism is the practice of sitting still and observing one's own mind. This practice can, of course, be taken up by Catholics, Jews, Muslims—with no need to convert to a new religion. Meditation can become part of anyone's life. I will often refer throughout this book to "sitting" or "sitting still," by which I mean the practice of seated meditation.

I hope this book is helpful for inmates. There is enough information here for a prisoner to start his or her own practice, whether or not teachers or other books are available. I also hope this book is helpful for those Buddhists outside prison walls who want to volunteer their time and energy to help inmates with their practice. More inmates inquire about Buddhism than there are people to answer their questions. I have tried to be both practical and realistic about the rewards and difficulties in store for those who want to work with inmates. I have been on both sides of the bars, and this has made me cautious and hopeful as I try to describe this work.

There is nothing corrective or healing about prisons in the United States. Inmates who want to change their lives and find peace are usually on their own. If personal change is to happen, it will be *in spite of* the prison environment. For most inmates, the whole process of arrest, indictment, trial, sentencing—and then the first entry into prison—is an experience of pure hell, a deep humiliation that brings with it fear, anger, and a sense of total powerlessness. Everything is being done to you. You have no say in how events will turn out. You are completely alone and can talk to no one (except, sometimes, an attorney) about what is happening to you.

So the question for someone entering prison for the first time is: How can I survive mentally, physically, and spiritually? How can I keep my humanity in a totally inhuman environment? How can I experience some sense of mastery when it looks like I'm totally powerless? Prisons are places of great suffering, violence, noise, hatred, and—every so often— friendship, laughter, and kindness. Although not entirely unlike the outside world, life in prison is more negative, intense, and unyielding than life outside.

Although meditation, compassion, and precept practice have helped me and many others get through our prison lives, these are not some "chicken soup" cure that will soothe every mental wound and pacify every emotional storm. If you are in prison, everything is *not* all right. And meditation itself can be difficult at times. To taste the deep peace meditation can offer requires nothing less than complete self-acceptance, an unflinching willingness to "sit with" our own mind and body—all the pain, suffering, and feelings of injury we hold within us. It requires interior discipline, something prisoners may think they lack. Discipline, in its external form, is imposed by the very structure of prison, but sitting still in silence is so out of keeping with the chaotic, noisy atmosphere of prison that it takes great courage and cleverness to practice at all. Practicing Buddhism in prison is an act of bravery, not an act of escape; it really means taking up the life of the warrior.

Sometimes meditation can be a great joy. It can be a big relief—a simple and effective stress-reduction technique and a means for bringing about deep transformation. Combined with Buddhist beliefs and guidelines for behavior, or any other time-tested ethical system, meditation can lead to the re-forming of one's mental, emotional, and ethical life. The practice can become a vehicle for lasting change. Yet there are obstacles and distractions. It is hard to sit still. It is hard to concentrate without drifting off into mind trips. It is hard to incorporate sitting into a daily routine.

I had the good fortune to discover and begin practicing Buddhist meditation more than a decade before my prison experience. My meditation practice, obviously, had not made me perfect and I had long neglected to commit myself to the core behavioral precepts of Buddhism. Meditation had at that time seemed trippy and exotic; changes in consciousness it dealt with made it seem similar to, if more benign than, the drugs and alcohol that had been part of my lifestyle. Still, on entering prison, I was fortunate to have some of the tools of Buddhism at my disposal.

My experience with Buddhist practice is mostly within the Zen and vipassana traditions of North America. *Zen* is a Japanese word derived from the Chinese term *Ch'an,* which refers to focused, sitting meditation. Vipassana, sometimes called "insight meditation," is a North American lay tradition descended from Burmese and Sri Lankan monastic Buddhism, sometimes known as "theravadan." The bias of my own experience will be reflected in this book.

From the third century B.C.E. until now, Buddhism has accumulated an ocean of history, traditions, and practices extending through the cultures of India, Nepal, Tibet, China, Vietnam, and many other countries. No one can know all its history or all the complications of its numerous sects. What I find interesting to watch is Buddhism's current transformation in North America and Europe. And this transformation in the U.S. religious landscape is starting to find its way into our prisons.

RELIGIOUS FREEDOM IN U.S. PRISONS

Most U.S. prisons are unfriendly to any faith tradition that is not mainstream Christianity. Christian chaplains have a long, entrenched position in our prison systems. Judaism and Islam have only recently won the right to have official chaplains in a few prisons, and this right came after lengthy legal battles by non-Christian prisoners, especially Jewish, Black Muslim, and Native American inmates.

One of the earliest of these battles was actually concerned with Buddhism. In 1967, a Texas inmate wrote to a Shin Buddhist minister in San Francisco, Reverend Hogen Fujimoto. Writing from the headquarters of the Buddhist Churches of America, as the Shin sect is known in the United States, Fujimoto carried on a lone ministry to U.S. inmates between the years 1963 and 1979. He began a correspondence with an inmate known as Cruz, but the prison administrators did not approve of Cruz's enthusiasm for an "exotic" religion. They refused to let him correspond with Fujimoto or to use the prison's chapel. For several months they locked Cruz in isolation; two slices of bread were the only food he was given each day. Cruz filed a lawsuit, which he originally had to write

17

on prison toilet paper. The case, known as *Cruz v. Beto,* went all the way to the U.S. Supreme Court and was decided in the inmate's favor in 1977. It became a foundational law case in issues of religious freedom for American inmates. [1]

The state of Washington only recently hired a part-time Buddhist chaplain, a man whose religious name is Dharmachari Aryadaka, who may be the first such chaplain in the United States. Despite such progress, a pronounced bias still exists against Buddhism on the part of U.S. prison administrators and the chaplains' bureaucracy.

Of the two million people behind bars in the United States, 90 percent are men. One out of every 147 U.S. residents is in a jail or prison. African-Americans outnumber whites seven to one. Among Hispanic men between the ages of twenty and thirty, 4 percent are in prison. Among white men of the same age group, 1.5 percent are in prison. More than 40 percent of inmates never completed high school. Prisons are a reflection of the racism and class structure that the United States likes to pretend doesn't exist.

Because of mandatory sentencing laws, such as "three strikes, you're out," U.S. prisons are overcrowded to such an extent that more than one in four state prisons is now operated under some sort of court order or consent decree—legal remedies that require the institutions to comply with constitutional and legal guidelines for safe and humane operation. Sometimes the federal courts have ordered that prison administrations be taken away from states or counties and turned over to independent corporations who are accountable only to the courts. Sometimes the courts have had to order institutions to stop admitting new inmates or to discharge those already there.

Meanwhile, new prison construction proceeds unchallenged, and inmates have become a valuable commodity in the new private-sector prison economy. Prisoners are often shipped across state lines, far from family and local support systems, to fill up "rent-a-prisons," facilities supplied by large, multibillion-dollar businesses, such as the Wackenhut Corporation or the megaprison operation known as the Corrections Corporation of America.

These corporations have no incentive to reduce recidivism—the reincarceration rate of released inmates—so treatment and education programs that might improve prisoners chances of success on the outside are not a priority. Prison corporations are invested in the economic advantage of keeping a good supply of warm bodies with long sentences. What inmates are allowed to do educationally and religiously during their time inside is often up to local administrators. No particular programs or privileges—visitation, letter writing, religious instruction—are guaranteed to inmates by the U.S. Constitution. Federal and state prison systems often have regulations that change constantly and that may be enforced or not, depending on the whims of administrators.

For many years, the U.S. court system was completely silent about the religious rights of prisoners. Although the First Amendment of the Constitution states that "Congress shall make no law respecting an establishment of religion or prohibiting the free exercise thereof," convicted felons have often been considered civilly dead. Many states have treated inmates as having no constitutional rights, such as the right to vote or to freely practice their religions.

In ruling on the *Cruz v. Beto* case, the Supreme Court indicated that the First Amendment *does* guarantee the free exercise of religion to prisoners. This case, plus the legal efforts of the Native American Church and of Black Muslims in the 1960s and 1970s, helped make it clear that non-Christian inmates must be accorded some rights within U.S. penal institutions. But in practice, *some* rights is the operative phrase—not *equal* rights with Christian inmates.

After the *Cruz v. Beto* decision, some lower court rulings reinterpreted this Supreme Court precedent by allowing prisons to prohibit religious activities if there were a "rational basis" for such restrictions. As anyone who has been around prisons could predict, the rational basis most frequently cited by prison administrators has been security.

This "rational basis" criterion, originating in a 1990 nonprison case called *Employment Division v. Smith*, worried many religious leaders. Congress was lobbied, which resulted in the 1993 passage of the Religious

19

Freedom Restoration Act (RFRA). This law stipulated that, instead of rational bases, "compelling state interest" was required before the freedom to practice religion could be restricted—a higher standard. Unfortunately, the U.S. Supreme Court, ruling on a case called *Boerne v. Flores,* struck down the RFRA in an August 1997 decision, which meant that the extent to which prisons must accommodate a diversity of beliefs is again open to interpretation. In September 2000, President Clinton signed a compromise law called the Religious Liberty Protection Act, written to address the Supreme Court's objections to the RFRA. More litigation will surely follow.

Bo Lozoff, author of *We Are All Doing Time* and founder of the Prison Ashram Project, describes changes he has seen since beginning his prison work in the 1970s: "During the 25 years that I have been working in prisons, the national budget for building and operating prisons has gone from $500 million to $31 billion per year. The number of institutions has quadrupled. . . . One out of every 50 children in the United States now has a parent in prison. More young black males are now in prison than in college. Our own mailing list has grown from a few dozen dharma seekers to over 30,000." [2]

After Reverend Fujimoto's pioneering work in the 1960s and 1970s, other Buddhist groups in the United States began to work with inmates. Zen Mountain Monastery, in upstate New York, started prison work at Sing Sing in 1984. The Prison Dharma Network was founded by then-inmate Fleet Maull in 1989. Other Buddhist teachers, like Robert Aitken Roshi in Hawaii and Tenshin Reb Anderson, former co-abbot of Zen Center in San Francisco, began writing to or visiting with individual inmates. Most sects of Buddhism frown on aggressive, missionary kinds of religious promotion, so that Buddhist prison programs began haphazardly, usually in response to requests from inmates looking for instruction. Buddhist teachers and centers who tried to respond to these initial requests faced many difficulties; I will discuss these in more detail in chapter 3.

HOLDING BACK DISASTER

Even with institutional problems, interest in Buddhist meditation practice has grown tremendously in the dorms and cellblocks of U.S. prisons.

Why is this so? Perhaps it's because so little that is new or interesting goes on in the correctional systems to engage the intellectual or spiritual needs of inmates. The U.S. prison system has become a metal and concrete wasteland, a desert littered with discarded educational and rehabilitation programs, abandoned in the new era of hard-line, punitive sentencing policies. Violence and racism are tacitly allowed to flourish, and thousands of human beings shrivel and die spiritually and emotionally in our prisons while those in power look the other way.

Yet deserts often produce hermits—fierce spiritual explorers who thrive in the harsh and lonely heat. The word "hermit" actually comes from the Greek word for "desert," *eremos,* and our western contemplative tradition owes its existence to pioneer desert fathers, brave eccentric hermits like St. Anthony, who blazed spiritual trails for Christianity in its first thousand years.

In Buddhist tradition, hermits have tended to live in mountains and forests. Isolation of any kind, even imprisonment, leaves one alone with one's own mind. Isolation can be a curse or a blessing. Although there is a lot of human contact in prisons, that contact is often icy and distant, in the case of guards, and untrustworthy or dangerous, in the case of other inmates. Even with five people in the same cell, prison life can be lonely and isolating—socially, sexually, and emotionally. It is noisy, anxiety-producing, and very stark. Prisoners feel cut off from family, friends, and the ordinary daily realities of people outside. Separation from custodial staff—who are trained in the art of distancing and who often become apathetic or exquisitely cruel—is sharply defined. Isolation from other inmates is sustained by the aura of distrust and fear that pervades the prison environment. Friends and family often stop writing and stop visiting. People who live outside prison walls may think that fear is the predominant emotion in prisons, and this may be true at first.

But most inmates will admit that loneliness becomes the most pervasive and oppressive feeling of all.

When someone is alone with her or his own mind, that mind's unruly nature starts to show itself. Sometimes the mind can act as a generator of negative and destructive thoughts. Prisoners facing this challenge have two choices. They can plunge into distractions—such as gossip, the underground prison economy, television, drugs, and card games—or they can make another, braver, choice: to face the mind directly and befriend it.

Facing, accepting, and learning to love and forgive one's own mind is the essence of meditation. Being left alone with a chattering, chaotic mind may be one reason inmates are increasingly attracted to meditation—which, at its core, is a practice that can tame and calm the mind and educate the emotions. In fact, the practice of sitting still and observing the mind predates Buddhism. It existed in the yogic traditions of India as early as 3000 B.C.E., and many kinds of meditation have been developed in other religions around the world. Buddhism, which focuses on one's own experience rather than on adherence to a system of beliefs, may be attractive to those who are uncomfortable with the dogmas of institutional religions. Many inmates had poor early experiences with religion and are very cautious about getting involved with any organized belief system. Prisoners often view themselves as outlaws or rebels, and part of that rebellion may be against the excessive moralisms or promotion of illogical beliefs they saw in the religions of their childhoods. There is no God to rebel against in Buddhism and no hierarchy to submit to. The historical Buddha never claimed either divinity or infallibility. He taught that people must make their own spiritual decisions based on direct experience.

Arturo Esquel, an inmate at Pelican Bay Prison in Northern California, tells how he came upon Buddhism in prison:

One day a friend of mine lent me a book written by a Japanese samurai master about Zen, and it really went to my heart. One thing he said had a strong effect on me: Man yearns for what is true on earth, for only by finding truth will he put an end to the restlessness and find within himself the foundation he seeks. And: Buddhist practitioners aspire to place themselves in the same responsive relationship with the universe as did the Buddha and Jesus, so that they may experience it firsthand. It was the first time I had ever even heard about Buddhism, and I was eager to learn more. I asked my friend what Buddhism was, but he didn't know. He said that he had heard that Buddhists were very disciplined and dedicated people. [3]

Esquel's mention of both Buddha and Jesus reminds me that some Buddhist teachers in America and Europe advise their western students against abandoning the religions of their upbringing too quickly. All spiritual traditions deserve careful study, and many Buddhist practices may be helpful to people who continue in other religions. My own teacher for many years, Robert Aitken Roshi, counts among his teaching heirs a Lutheran minister, a Catholic priest, and a Catholic nun.

Bo Lozoff, who has been teaching meditation practices in U.S. prisons for a quarter of a century, also cautions against sectarian narrowness in teaching spiritual practices in prisons. He discusses the word *dharma*, which, when capitalized, is often taken to refer exclusively to the Buddha's teaching. "The word *dharma* is not just a Buddhist term. It's also Hindu, and its original meaning is 'that which holds back disaster.' So any spiritual practice that promotes compassion and helps us train our mind can be considered dharma. Any solid spiritual tradition can help us hold back disaster. This is not about converting people. When I met with His Holiness the Dalai Lama to explain our prison work to him, he twice leaned over to me and said, 'I hope you're not pushing Buddhism.' He was very clear about this." [4] What a good way of describing practice in prison—holding back disaster.

THE BUDDHA MEETS A CRIMINAL

Prisons as we know them did not exist in the time of the historical Buddha. Indeed, they did not exist in the West, in any form familiar to us, until the eighteenth century. Before that time, in both the Orient and the West, punishment for crimes was handled in a number of more non-institutional ways—mostly by swiftly accomplished executions. Banishment, disfigurement, and slavery were other common punishments.

Castles sometimes contained dungeons, of course, but they were mostly for prisoners of war or kidnapees being held for ransom or to be sold into slavery. A slave economy ringed the Mediterranean well before the New World was discovered and even before the dawn of the Roman Empire; dungeons existed as warehouses and distribution centers for this market. But the idea of serving a defined amount of time in prisons as we know them now is actually quite a recent human innovation.

Prince Siddhartha Gautama, who was born about 530 B.C.E. in the area we now call Nepal, had a famous encounter with a criminal during his teaching career. Angulimala was a notorious murderer feared by everyone in the kingdom—everyone except the man called the *Buddha* ("The One Who Is Awake"). The story of their encounter appears in the *Angulimala Sutta*, one of the 152 sutras in the midlength collection of the Pali-language canon. The Pali word *sutta*, (or *sutra* in Sanskrit), refers to the Buddhist scriptures, words said to have come from the Buddha himself. This body of work was set down in writing about five centuries after the Buddha's lifetime.

The *Angulimala Sutta* describes the confrontation between the Buddha and Angulimala, a ferocious serial killer. After he recognized "the awakened one," Angulimala was astonished that this holy man did not turn and run away in terror like everyone else. After some verbal dueling and many excuses from Angulimala for his evil ways, the notorious criminal was overcome by Prince Gautama's logic and compassion. He finally burst into tears and asked for the Buddha's help. The wandering holy man taught Angulimala the Four Noble Truths and the Eightfold Path, a program for change that he advised for everyone—monks, nuns, or householders. The Buddha eventually even ordained Angulimala as a monk, much to the shock of some of the other monks. The importance of the Angulimala story for us is that it makes quite clear that criminals were not to be excluded from the sangha, the community of the Buddha's followers, or from the possibility of awakening.

Another notorious criminal figure, in later Buddhist history, was the eleventh-century Mongolian, Jetsun Milarepa. A murderer and practitioner of black magic, Milarepa was able to turn his life around after discovering the dharma in the person of the Tibetan teacher Marpa. Through an intensive lifelong practice, Milarepa was able to repattern his negative personality traits—deviousness, violence, and deception—into skillful and charismatic teaching methods. He was thus able to bring many of his contemporaries to states of mental clarity and release from suffering. Milarepa is still revered as a saint in the Tibetan and Mongolian Buddhist traditions.

A PLAN FOR CHANGE

Although, like most religions, Buddhism recommends avoiding evil and doing good, its emphasis is on suffering and liberation from suffering. This is a very different tactic than the approach of religions that focus on sin and salvation from sin. This emphasis on suffering and release is, I think, another reason why Buddhism may be appealing to many inmates, who are certainly familiar with the experience of suffering.

The Four Noble Truths, the Eightfold Path, and the five lay precepts are the main elements of the program that the historical Buddha designed after his own enlightenment under the bodhi tree. He wanted others to reach the same state of deliverance from suffering.

The following outlines the framework of what the historical Buddha discovered and the program used to train (or retrain) Angulimala, Milarepa, and every Buddhist follower since those times. These principles are the context within which the practice of meditation works as a complete Buddhist program for the Great Recovery. They identify what we need to experience and what we need to put into action in order to live fully as Buddhists:

THE FOUR NOBLE TRUTHS

I.   Suffering exists.

II.   There is an origin of suffering.

III.   There can be an end to suffering.

IV.   There is a release from the causes of suffering, Buddha called this release the Eightfold Path.

THE NOBLE EIGHTFOLD PATH

1. right view
2. right intention
3. right speech
4. right action
5. right livelihood
6. right effort
7. right mindfulness
8. right concentration

The Eightfold Path—especially right speech, action, and livelihood—may be achieved through a commitment to follow the five lay precepts, a concrete guide for the lives of all Buddha's followers. Nuns and monks take additional vows, but these five precepts are the central, bottom-line principles of Buddhist ethical behavior:

THE FIVE LAY PRECEPTS

1. Not killing
2. Not taking what is not given
3. Not speaking harmfully
4. Not abusing or trafficking in alcohol or drugs
5. Not engaging in abusive sexual behavior

And there you have it: the whole of Buddhism. Yet countless books have been written to explain these simple lists. One of them, Stephen Batchelor's book *Buddhism Without Beliefs,* makes clear that the Four Noble Truths are not just noble; they are "ennobling" to those who experience them. Batchelor also insists that these ennobling truths are not a four-part doctrine to be believed but, rather, are realities to be experienced. In other words, we let ourselves experience the fact that life is *anguish* (Batchelor's replacement for the word "suffering"), and we personally discover the origin of anguish in craving, sometimes translated from the Pali word *tanha* as "clinging." Then we move on to practice the eight active principles of the Buddhist path in our own life circumstances. It is in this practice of the Eightfold Path that we begin to experience the cessation, the disappearance—only momentarily at first—of anguish, ignorance, and craving.

An Ohio Buddhist inmate, Gunaratna Sarika, says that Buddhism focuses its attention on our present circumstances and on the release from the causes of suffering we find there. This is why he was first attracted to Buddhism after incarceration. For Sarika, Buddhism "does not base its teachings on metaphysical questions such as: What is the origin of man? or What is the meaning of life? And it does not endorse or even renounce the existence of God or gods. It focuses its attention on the here and now." [5]

The Four Ennobling Truths are often explained by a medical analogy. The first truth, that suffering exists, is like a doctor's initial diagnosis of a patient. The second is a statement of the etiology, the source, of the illness: There is an origin of suffering. The prognosis is that there can be an end to suffering (the third truth). The fourth truth is the prescription, the Eightfold Path. This four-part procedure identifies our constant unhappiness, anguish, or suffering as a result of our untrained mind and emotions, which constantly push and pull us with distorted thoughts and emotional cravings—hatreds, fears, and jealousies. We are always trying to hold on to things or notions that we think will give us comfort. Sometimes we try to push things away—thoughts, people, or objects; this is the strategy of denial or avoidance. This twin process of attraction and aversion, infatuation and hatred, grasping and pushing away—this is what gets us into trouble.

We try to make things hold still, but nothing stays the same for long. The friend who wrote faithfully, no longer keeps in touch. The girlfriend who pledged undying love in her last letter did not show up for visitation last Sunday. The guard who was decent and fair is soon transferred to another unit. Our own bodies keep changing as well, and will soon enough take us into sickness, old age, and death. Life is change, and we don't like it! Like spoiled children, we cling to some notion of how we think things should be, and we are constantly disappointed.

The Buddha explained that our clinging to things, ideas, emotions, and people is what makes us suffer. And he offered us a way out. The Noble Eightfold Path is a list of behaviors, attitudes, and practices that, when put together as a program for living, will release us from the origins of suffering, whether we are in prison or in the so-called free world.

A BRIEF VERSION OF THE EIGHTFOLD PATH

RIGHT VIEW, the first of the eight paths, means that we keep our mind on the Four Noble Truths and on our commitment to the Buddha's program for change. Right view means, in the Buddha's own words, that we should concentrate on "the ideas that are fit for attention." This means ideas like impermanence (things are always changing), no-self (one of the Buddha's most radical and difficult-to-understand teachings, which I'll discuss later in this chapter), compassion, peacemaking, cause and effect (*karma*), and the interrelationship of all things (more technically called "dependent co-arising"). Right view, at its simplest, means, "Keep your eyes on the path."

RIGHT INTENTION refers to the motivation that results from right view. We resolve not to harm but to commit ourselves to compassion and goodwill. We resolve and commit ourselves to the Great Recovery. Our intention is to position ourselves toward the truth, not because we want to be better than someone else, or have more power or insight, but because this is the most real thing we could possibly commit ourselves to doing.

RIGHT SPEECH means not lying. It also means that we understand speech to have consequences—it can be used to harm or to heal others. Even more subtle is the Buddha's suggestion that we not use speech to make ourselves right and others wrong. For example, we should not argue with a Mormon inmate to prove that Buddhism is better than his or her religion. Right speech also means not participating in gossip and not using words as our vehicle for anger or jealousy.

RIGHT ACTION means that we commit ourselves to following the Buddhist precepts of not killing, not stealing, not engaging in sexual misconduct, and so forth. In the *Anguttara Nikaya Sutra,* the Buddha is quoted as saying that right action means "dwelling with club laid down, with knife laid down." Right action is non-violent and means that we train ourselves not to act from automatic, self-serving motives; after much training, we eventually learn to move in a world where peace and compassion have become as automatic as our former negative impulses.

RIGHT LIVELIHOOD commits the person who wants to be released from the causes of suffering to engage only in honest, nonharmful work. It means, in the strict traditional sense, no trading in meat, weapons, living beings, intoxicants, or poisons. Right livelihood also means that we avoid work that involves deception, like sorcery, fortune-telling, or selling used cars in a dishonest way. More thoroughly observed, it is also a commitment to nonextravagance (unlike the corporate CEO who earns many millions of dollars a year while others in his company barely earn a living wage). Right livelihood essentially means that all Buddhists— whether nuns, monks, or laity—should make their livings in ways that do not harm or deceive other beings. We should all live simply and be generous to others.

RIGHT EFFORT is like the so-called maintenance steps in self-help programs such as Alcoholics Anonymous or Narcotics Anonymous. It reminds us to maintain our commitment to the path we have chosen. The Buddha likened right effort to the fine-tuning of a stringed instrument. Too tightly strung, we become fanatical and inflexible in our religious behavior. Yet a string that is too loose is not good either; too loose, we become lazy about our training and neglectful of the precepts.

RIGHT MINDFULNESS means staying focused, throughout all daily activities, on the workings of our mind. Mindfulness is the effort to extend meditation into the daily realm of our speech, thought, and behavior. It is a commitment to be alert, to pay attention to the people and things around us. In the *Samyutta Nikaya*, a sutra in the midlength Pali-language collection, the Buddha demonstrates right mindfulness with an image. Pretend, he said, that you are carrying a jar of oil balanced on your head. And pretend that you are walking between a stage on which a beauty queen is performing and a crowd driven mad by her enticements. Pretend as well, as a further inducement to caution, that behind you walks an enforcer with a sword, who is ready to behead you should even a drop of oil spill from the pot on your head. "Thus you should train," the Buddha concluded. Training for this kind of alertness to the world can only come from meditation, the core of the Buddha's training methods.

RIGHT CONCENTRATION or meditation, is supported by the seven previous paths. It cannot be accomplished without them, nor can they be kept in motion without the energy and clarity generated by meditation. Right concentration, which will be explained in more detail in the next chapter, means learning to exist in the present time and place—the famous "here and now." Meditation trains us to become observers of ourselves and, eventually, to experience our thoughts and emotions with equanimity; that is, with no clinging to and no judgments about those thoughts and emotions. Meditation is not sedation. It is, rather, a special kind of compassionate alertness to ourselves, to others, and to the whole universe. Right concentration means sitting still and watching the loud, confused, and busy parade of thoughts as they pass through our consciousness of the present moment.

For prisoners, as well as for all other Buddhist practitioners, the Four Noble Truths and the Eightfold Path are available and ready to be explored. Many inmates seem attracted to the logic, simplicity and practicality of the Buddha's outline for the end of suffering. Gunaratna Sarika told me about his experience: "Being raised within the doctrines of Roman Catholicism, I was never given such a simple formula as has been provided to me through the teachings of the Buddha. For me, all that I was able to get out of Catholicism were unknowable, unreachable solutions to life's many bumps. I was never provided with a treatment for this life, such as is found in the Four Noble Truths." [6]

The relevance of Buddhist teaching and methods does not mean that there are not good training methods and deep contemplative traditions in the three major western monotheisms—Judaism, Islam, and Christianity. There are. The problem is that these techniques of training in the contemplative traditions were marginalized over time and restricted to monks, nuns, and other religious specialists. Laypeople were left with little to do except sing hymns and donate money. The monotheisms gave their adherents a great deal to believe (often requiring unquestioning faith). But people were often given little to do. Buddhism, on the other hand, at least as it is being interpreted in North America, gives us a lot to do, without a lot to believe—and this may be the key to its increasing spread outside of Asia.

WHO?

The Eightfold Path—the eight elements of a plan for release from the causes of suffering—is not easy. Taking up this path is as life-changing as joining a gang or pledging loyalty to an organized crime group. But the Eightfold Path commits us to movement in the opposite direction. In a prison setting—where everything in the environment encourages violence, verbal abuse, scheming, and deception, a commitment to the path is a warrior's act of rebellion. (I don't like using the word "warrior," because it buys into the overly-macho prison culture, but it is the only word that seems strong enough to convey the courage needed to practice mindfulness, compassion and meditation in a prison.) Joan Halifax, a Buddhist teacher who has worked with a meditation program in a high-security New Mexico prison, writes:

> Inmates have to be so vigilant all the time, constantly defending themselves. In these conditions, they find it difficult to water the seeds of happiness. What we emphasize in the beginning of our practice with these men is the development of strength and compassion. I can't tell prisoners that every moment is wonderful. This is

31

simply not true, not in prison. First we need to learn to trust each other, and this takes strength, understanding, and kindness. With our emphasis on strength with silence and stillness, these men open up to a more insightful and compassionate response to the difficult world in which they find themselves. [7]

A variety of meditation exercises are given throughout the rest of this book—all adapted from various Buddhist traditions. Inmates new to Buddhism should try each one, then decide which forms are best suited to your own needs. The next chapter includes more details on meditation techniques, but for now, please try the following exercise as a way of introducing yourself to the practice of sitting still.

MEDITATION ONE: WHO IS SITTING?

Sit comfortably on a chair or on the side of the bed. Keep your feet flat on the floor and your back straight. Let your eyes blur as you look at some point in front of you. You don't need to close your eyes all the way.

Now pay attention to your breathing. Just notice each time you exhale. Notice what you hear in your environment: clanging doors, shouts, noises from radios and televisions. As you inhale, think of the word "who." As you exhale, think of the word "hears." Make this a continuing, breathing question: Who hears?

After a few minutes of this, begin to notice the feelings in your body: the feel of your feet on the floor, the pressure on your butt where you are sitting, the temperature of your skin, the tightness of any muscles, the feel of cloth against your body. Now inhale again and think "who" and exhale to the sound of the word "feels." Make this another in-and-out breathing question: Who feels? Continue this for a few minutes, staying aware of the sense of touch and temperature.

Now notice what comes into your brain from your eyes and ask, as you inhale, the question "who?" As you exhale, add the word "sees." Then, after a few minutes, do the same as you inhale and exhale, with smell. Who smells?

Notice the aromas you can identify as you breathe. Add taste to the breathing questions. Let each sense question absorb your breathing for a few minutes. Finally, just inhale silently and exhale to the sound of "who?" Keep up the question "who?" on each exhale for as long as you want. Then slowly bring your attention back to your surroundings. Stretch, stand up, and resume your usual activities.

There is no more important question in Buddhism, or in human life, for that matter, than the question *who?* Who is sitting here breathing? Who is trying to meditate? Who is it that has sight and smell, hearing and feeling? In Buddhist legend, the emperor of China asked the famous Indian Buddhist, Bodhidharma, "Who are you?" Bodhidharma replied honestly, "I don't know."

This sounds like a poor answer for such a famous meditation master to give. But it was not. Any one of us could respond truthfully with the same statement. It is a universal unanswered question in human life. It is this "I don't know" that puts everyone on the path in the first place. Bodhidharma went off to a cave and did sitting-still meditation—or what he called "wall-gazing"—for another nine years, just to find out.

Buddhist practice is an experimental method that tries to find the answer to the important *who* question. Buddhism provides no dogma that will give us an answer. There is a hint, however, in the Buddhist teaching of "no abiding self." So a preliminary answer to the question of who is sitting here might be: not who you always thought was here.

Like the historical Buddha, we must sit down, sit still, and start to find out. Once we start, we are already on the path.

REFORMING INSIDE

If we look at some of the words that have been used to describe prisons, we can find in their meanings some clues to the original purposes of these institutions. "Reformatory," a little archaic but still used sometimes to describe long-term juvenile facilities, gives us the idea that prisons are meant to *re-form* the values, attitudes, and behaviors of their residents. "Correction" is another term frequently used to describe the prison setting and its intentions. This is a concept similar to reform, the idea being that something in the inmate needs correction or change. "Penitentiary" refers to a place of repentance, where the hoped-for outcome is remorse and a turning away from previous behavior. Even from the earliest times in American prison history, chaplains were provided to prisoners with all these hopes for change in mind.

Today, punishment is the idea that most people equate with prisons, and prisons do indeed serve that function. Penology is the study of punishment. The penal codes list all the punishments for all the possible crimes in a given jurisdiction. Although the favored term these days for the prison industry is "correction," we are witnessing the growth of a system that operates with no theory of how to correct, reform, or bring repentance to individual prisoners. The current political climate in which U.S. prisons operate emphasizes security, confinement of inmates, and protection of the community. Rehabilitation is rarely on the agenda. This situation is not totally the fault of the system, surrounded as it is, by a broader political culture that offers few new ideas except for more and longer punishment. Even the social sciences (psychology, sociology, anthropology) have failed to give our culture, let alone our prison system, a workable method for human change.

Without support or new ideas from prison administrations, or from outside experts, the individual inmate is left alone to re-form herself or himself. But reform often seems only a vague possibility. Too many inmates are left to sink into more violence, resentment, and depression. For those who decide to try reform, sitting-still meditation can become a central practice, giving energy and clarity to the effort. But—as I will say many times throughout this book—meditation can be central to transformation, but it will never be the only thing that needs to be done. If individual inmates embrace the full implications of Buddhism—which include the Four Noble Truths, the Eightfold Path, and the five lay precepts—then true personal change can begin. But reform, like meditation, is never a done deal; it is a continuing practice, with times of difficulty followed by times when sitting still and practicing the precepts seem the easiest thing in the world. Change, always change.

Yet the whole Buddhist recipe for happiness and its program for personal reform will not be effective without accepting the other supports that are needed—adult education, therapy, medication, twelve-step programs. Real reform of self must take place with a core of spiritual values motivating other psychological and educational strategies for change. And such spiritual values do not necessarily have to come from Buddhism.

For inmates who want to change, I offer in this book many forms of Buddhist meditation techniques. For some inmates, these practices, undertaken as a regular part of daily life, will be enough to assist in the process of change. Meditation alone, free of any sectarian belief system, can still help train the mind and lower stress. But this book is also about being a Buddhist in prison, and I hope there is enough here for those prisoners who want to take up this ancient and rewarding path.

When I was released from prison, an inmate friend who is a dedicated Christian gave me a small carved and varnished pendant to wear around my neck. It was in the shape of a book, and he told me that it represented the Bible. (He had never understood what I did each morning, sitting on pillows on the floor of my cell. And I think he must have hoped that I would return to Christianity.) I didn't wear his gift at first because I was wary of its sectarian meaning. But gradually I changed my mind. Now I wear it every day. I decided it can just as well represent the Buddhist sutras. Each morning, after offering incense, I carefully put this pendant around my neck, where it stays for the rest of the day. I do this because it represents my prison friend's best intentions, and it reminds me of my own.

CHAPTER 1 NOTES

1. I am grateful to the research of J. Anthony Stultz and Virginia Cohn Parkum for the Reverend Fujimoto story.

2. Bo Lozoff, "A Nation Behind Bars," *Shambhala Sun,* March 1998, 15.

3. Arturo Esquel, "Searching for a Way to Leave No One Behind: The Transformation of a Mexican Gangster," *Mandala* (Soquel, Calif.: FPMT, Nov-Dec 1997), 43.

4. Lozoff, personal communication, 1998.

5. Gunaratna Sarika, personal communication, 1997.

6. Ibid.

7. Joan Halifax, personal communication, 1998.

Sitting Inside

Our practice is concerned with freedom and, for obvious reasons, this is very important to prisoners. It soon became clear that there were prisoners inside . . . who are really free, just as there are many so-called free people outside the prison who are really prisoners.[1]   —John Daido Loori

Former federal inmate Fleet Maull, who founded the Prison Dharma Network and is a contributor to this book, has been a student of both the Tibetan and the Zen lineages of Buddhism. Maull says that practicing inside a prison is like doing meditation in a *charnel ground*, a place where dead bodies are left to decompose and where vultures and other carrion fight with each other for their share of the remains.[2] This is a morbid but accurate analogy.

THE CONTEXT OF PRISON PRACTICE

An atmosphere of fear, rage, and shame pervades prisons. Interpersonal tensions are so high that the attempt to achieve any kind of serenity—let alone simple quiet—seems almost impossible. Such an environment of noise and negative emotions would be hard to duplicate anywhere else. Prisoners who want to practice Buddhism are faced with some real and difficult obstacles to meditation practice, difficulties that should not be minimized by anyone, especially Buddhist volunteers from outside.

Prisons are not monasteries; the intent and the atmosphere of the two institutions are quite different. But this comparison is often made nevertheless. In chapter 1, I mentioned some of the similarities between inmates and monks or hermits. Both ways of life involve lonely, desertlike conditions. Before proceeding to the nuts and bolts of meditation practice inside, I'd like to examine the part of that analogy relating to environment.

First of all, prisons differ widely in the specifics of their environments. In some places, each person has his or her own cell—as in the prototype of the Christian monastery. In other institutions, inmates are crowded several to a cell or live in large dormitories that may contain up to a hundred people in one enclosure. Privacy, as in some very strict monasteries, is almost always at a premium in prisons. In fact, penal theory in the eighteenth and nineteenth centuries—and even down to our present times—saw the ideal prison as a circular structure with all the cells open to a central tower, or *panopticon*, from which the guards could easily see into any cell in the institution.

Being watched, at even the most private moments—such as going to the bathroom or showering or sleeping—is one of the subtlest and most pervasive of the punishments endured by prisoners. A punitive lack of privacy is a major difference between a monastic institution and a prison. A more thorough discussion of this idea, and the history of penal theory in Europe and the United States, may be found in Michel Foucault's book *Discipline and Punish*.

Both penal institutions and convents or monasteries are removed from the world, and daily life moves to an internal, structured schedule. But again the two places differ radically: the monastery should be a voluntary removal from secular life, but a prison is not. The schedules of both institutions may, in a sense, be imposed from above, yet the monastic schedule has input from the community members and is a deliberate, chosen structure to make time for such activities as liturgy, contemplation, chanting, and spiritual reading. Prison schedules may have only one time per week when inmates may attend chapel functions, and this activity often requires special permission—it is not guaranteed to all inmates.

The prison schedule is based on security first and foremost, then on the completion of necessities like meals, exercise, and hygiene activities.

Almost all other activities—inside work, recreation, education, phone calls, and even family visitations—are considered optional privileges. For this reason, these privileges are often denied on the slightest pretext—usually because of one of twin excuses: security ("We're in a lock-down") or staffing ("We're understaffed today; no visitors!").

Despite these obstacles, some Buddhist inmates do feel it is possible to create an atmosphere that is at least semimonastic. Indiana state inmate Kerry J. Greenwell writes:

> Yes, I definitely do think that it is possible to build a healthy sangha within the walls of a prison environment. Even though there are ups and downs, in prisons as well as out in society, I believe that if we were allowed, that we could form a type of monastic atmosphere. All of our needs are met, i.e., food, clothing, and shelter. We don't have the responsibility of having to support a family, so I think renunciation in that respect would be easier. We could devote all our time to study and practice, which, in turn, would not only benefit us but ultimately all of society, because if our practice is faithful in here, we could not help but become better human beings.[3]

But there is still a difference. The concept of renunciation is viewed in Buddhism as a voluntary act that is required especially of nuns and monks. They are expected to leave home—in classic Buddhist literature, monks and nuns are often called "home-leavers"—and they are expected to leave behind all attachments to material things. The home-leaving involved in going to prison, however, is not voluntary, and it is the court system that has ordered the renunciation. However, a prison economy does exist, much of it underground, so that it is possible to renounce attachments to the few material things that are available. Lama Yontan Gonpa, of the Padma Ling Center in Spokane, Washington, has a good deal of experience working with prisoners. He agrees that it is possible to change the context of prison practice by reimagining it as a monastery or as an opportunity for individual retreat. "You can look at incarceration as a retreat funded by the state, or you can look at it as a hell. It's your choice," he says.[4]

Greenwell also affirms this interior choice about life inside. "I'm sure that you know how easy it is to get caught up in the system and develop the 'prison mentality' that can lead to all sorts of suffering. My practice has kept me from falling victim to that type of mindset and has kept me grounded in reality. I've become more mature in my thinking, and developed a more compassionate life-view. I no longer blame others for my problems but realize that *I* am the source of my problems."[5]

Buddhist practice anywhere, inside or out, is about this "I" question. On entering prison, most inmates are only left with this forever-chattering "I." The simple distraction of choices, like what to wear today, or what movie to go to, or who to call on the phone—all these are removed. Moving from place to place, socializing at work or with family and friends—these distractions are suddenly gone. The newly arrived inmate experiences an involuntary renunciation of the toys of everyday life. More-established prisoners often have radios or televisions in their cells, which can serve to distract them from the experience of chattering mind, but of course this is only one kind of chatter replacing another. So the newly entering prisoner is in a kind of shock—left alone with her or his own thoughts. For the most part, these thoughts can be divided into "I want" and "I don't want" kinds of statements. For instance, "I want a cigarette," or "I don't want to play dominos." Many identity statements also arise, such as "I am Latino," or "I am misunderstood," as well as emotions: mostly fear, jealousy, and anger. Emotions are not as easy to identify and catch in the mental experience as are the more explicit, verbal thoughts.

And, of course, in prisons there is no one to talk to about any of this, because to explain it to another is to admit to weakness.

Most people, whether they are inmates or not, try to keep their attention outside their heads through activities and external distractions, so an end to these distractions can be a severe shock. Thus, outer-directed noise, aggression, or interpersonal manipulation often become the activities of the newly imprisoned person. It is as if inmates need noise in their outside environment in order to keep them from facing the fears and anxieties of undistracted interior experience.

San Quentin death-row inmate, writer, and Buddhist practitioner Jarvis Masters writes of a noisy new cell neighbor called Bosshog, whom Masters was gradually able to help calm down. Although this inmate never fully took up formal meditation, he was still able to learn some peaceful "self-talk" from Masters and was thankful for it when he completed his sentence. "When Bosshog was finally released from San Quentin some eighteen months later, he stood in front of my cell before leaving, and he and I smiled at each other, trying not to say good-bye. Almost in the same breath, we repeated what had become his favorite mantra whenever he felt he was about to blow his top: 'Man, man . . . if we are peaceful, if we are happy, we can smile, and everyone in our family, our entire society, will benefit from our peace.'" [6]

In prison, meditation must be practiced *despite* the setting and often without the intentional support of peers or the institutional authorities. Talking about the distractions he finds at Folsom Prison in California, inmate Paul Dewey has developed a very realistic attitude about the prison environment. He notes that for awhile he felt that "all the distractions were preventing me from getting maximum results from a weak practice. But if the distractions were preventing me from maintaining focus, then I was the problem, not the distractions. Toilet flushing, tier to tier shouting, and general cellblock chaos have never prevented me from staying focused on *Baywatch* or an old Santana song. And for me to expect that everyone and everything should grind to a halt just to accommodate my practice sessions, when they don't give a rat's ass about ANYTHING, then my expectations are unrealistic; I am setting up my practice for failure." [7] So the setting of any practice, inside prison or out, is often beyond our control. Instead of opposing these distractions, or hiding from them, the point of meditation practice is to learn to make skillful use of these circumstances as the raw material of our sitting-still experience.

WHY MEDITATE?

In chapter 1 we asked the question "Why Buddhism?" Now we turn to a more specific question about the central practice of Buddhism: Why meditate? The two questions are not the same, as meditation techniques can be used by anyone, Buddhist or not.

I would answer the first question by saying that living as a Buddhist—which includes the practice of meditation—also presumes commitment to the Eightfold Path and to the precepts. It is a total package. From a strictly Buddhist perspective, the continued practice of meditation should lead eventually to a dropping away of the small, individual "self" and a realization of the greater unity of self and world, a unity that thirteenth-century Zen teacher Eihei Dôgen called "the great whole." [8] The Chinese meditation teacher Foxin Bencai describes this dropping away or realization experience this way: "The flower of mind will suddenly burst into bloom." It is "like forgetting, then suddenly remembering; like being sick, then all of a sudden recovering." [9]

Aside from providing the opportunity for the kind of transcendent experience described by the old masters, what else can meditation do? What else can someone hope to achieve by sitting still to meditate? Will it help? And, if so, what exactly will it help *with?*

I was once visiting my brother, who lived in Paris. We went to dinner one night with some of his friends; a woman who was a Jungian analyst was sitting next to me. She had heard from my brother that I was Buddhist, and she was very curious about this. So she leaned over earnestly and asked me, "Since you've been meditating for more than twenty years, what results have you seen?" I felt stumped by such a simple question and blurted out, "Oh, when I meditate I end up feeling like doing the dishes and cleaning up my place."

For months I felt I had disappointed her—and myself—by not coming up with a deeper answer, something more psychological or spiritual that would capture the attention of a French intellectual. Later, I mentioned this incident to a Buddhist inmate with whom I talk each week. He said he thought my answer was a good one, and I see now that he is right. It was a statement of the very ordinariness of meditation, how it helps us focus mindfully on the details of daily life. One of the Zen ancestors described this simple truth as "Cutting wood and carrying water."

What then is meditation from a non-Buddhist, nonspiritual point of view?—in psychological and physiological terms only. Because meditation is an exercise in attention, you begin to learn to pay attention to the state of your body and the state of your mind. By trying to stay focused on breathing, or on a sound, or on a single image or thought, the person who meditates is learning to control mental attention—which conversely means learning to discover when you are distracted and to recover focus quickly.

This process of deliberate attention also develops what I call the *observer* level of mind. By this I mean that the person meditating soon learns to look down on her or his mental and emotional processes—as if from a platform above the self—and to gain a bit of detachment from these shifting moods and thoughts. In other words, you learn to notice such things as, "Oh, my thoughts are racing today," or, "It looks like I'm groggy and depressed right now." A great deal of psychological skill is gained by observing and accepting these shifting states. You are freed, in a sense, from being caught inside the mood or inside the frustration of scattered thoughts. The repeated exercise of this experience of observation also leads to greater emotional honesty with yourself, if not with others.

I don't know for certain that this has been measured scientifically, but most people who meditate report that they have much more energy—and a sense of emotional balance—on the days they sit still and do the practice. This may have been what I was trying to express to the French psychiatrist when I told her I was more apt to do the dishes willingly when I meditate. Like people who talk about the benefits of running, people who meditate notice these effects best in their absence—on a day they skip their practice of meditation or of running. Other physiological characteristics associated with meditation include lowered blood pressure, the production of relaxing alpha waves in the brain, and a general slowing of metabolic functions. To find out more about the physiological effects of meditation, and about the concept of secular meditation, consult Dr. Herbert Benson's book, *The Relaxation Response.*[10] In a prison setting, these possible psychological and physiological benefits of meditation can be very important, not only for the re-forming of the emotional life of an individual inmate, but also for the whole prison community, as inmates who meditate experience increased emotional honesty and control and decreased levels of emotional and physical stress. The practice of meditation itself is a perfectly legitimate undertaking that can also relieve suffering—by reducing bodily stress and by calming mental activity.

Meditation also functions as a method to confront our own mind—our "self," or what Dôgen called "the real dragon." But without the context of the rest of Buddhist practice, the secular meditator is left with the question of what to do after observing the workings of what many Buddhist teachers like to call "monkey mind," a mind that swings from tree to tree, with no apparent rhyme or reason.

SITTING STILL

Now let's look at how to do some simple Buddhist meditation practices in prison. Remember that Buddhism is a method, not a system of dogma. That's why the word *practice* is used so often. Meditation is a practice—something done over and over again—something, like music, that you can never do perfectly, but that you can always keep trying to improve. There are plenty of books available that cover the basic techniques and concepts behind Buddhist meditation; I've listed some of these on the reading list at the end of this book.

For the benefit of inmates who have only *Sitting Inside,* I will do my best to outline some practices that can be done with no guidance except your own inner commitment, your own beginner's mind. You can begin meditation whether or not there is a teacher or meditation instructor available to your institution. At a later point, it is important to get direction, if possible, either through direct visitations by an outside teacher or through teacher contact by phone or mail. Checking local phone directories (usually under "Churches, Buddhist") might also produce leads to teachers who work near a particular prison.

The simplest way I can describe meditation is to say that it is the practice of sitting still. To physically accomplish this stillness, a millennium of yoga—extending back even before the time of the historical Buddha—led to the development of the lotus position. This classic cross-legged, feet-on-thighs, yogic form is the ideal for sitting meditation. The best position, according to yogic tradition, is lying flat on your back, because the body is totally supported with no muscle strain. The problem, of course, is that this position is also our usual one for sleep and easily leads to that state. And here is an important point: meditation is not sedation or trance. It should be a combination of relaxation and alertness. Alertness is needed to keep the back straight and the head from nodding, and it is this vigilance that keeps people from falling asleep. If you do begin to doze, your body will automatically correct itself by waking you before you fall forward.

Most westerners can't manage a full-lotus position without a lot of time devoted to stretching exercises. What is most important initially is to find a way of sitting that raises the buttocks and leaves the knees pointed downward at about a 30-degree angle with the back straight. A meditation cushion, or *zafu,* is the usual solution to get this correct propping of the rear and the correct downward angle of the upper legs. But prison administrations often find reasons to keep zafus out their institutions. They are said to be an easy way to conceal contraband and are a danger to security. Some prisons do allow them in but often require that they be kept locked in chapel facilities and used only during the scheduled group meditation sessions—which may only be held once or twice a week. In other institutions, Buddhist prisoners have been allowed zafus in their cells.

Sitting Inside

But it is important not to let the zafu/no-zafu situation hinder you from beginning to practice. You don't need a zafu; you don't need incense; you don't need a Buddha image; you don't have to accomplish full lotus. All would be nice, and some prison sanghas have been able to put together very complete Buddhist dojos (meditation halls), including fish drums and candles and gongs and bells and wooden clappers. Access to these accessories depends on many variables, like the availability of outside help, institutional donation policies, and the attitudes of prison chaplains and administrators. Getting these things often depends on the hustle-ability and persistence of inmates themselves.

Most inmates who don't have access to zafus use folded-up blankets and pillows to support their sitting. This is fine. Try sitting at first in the half-lotus position, which is cross-legged with the left foot placed against the right thigh. If you can't do that comfortably, start with a simple cross-legged posture or with the supported kneeling posture, called *seiza* in Japanese. Experiment at first until you find the most comfortable and stable position for yourself.

NOISE, INSIDE AND OUT

Most meditation instruction books start with a sentence like, "Find a quiet place where you won't be disturbed." A good idea, but not always possible in the prison environment. Choosing a time and place for sitting still may often require a good deal of ingenuity and experimentation inside prisons. Some prisoners have their own cells, which makes the setting easier; others live in dorms or shared cells, which require a bit more creativity. Time is also important. Most prisoners choose either early morning or evening, after lights out, to do their sitting practice. Noise levels are lower at these times, and the self-consciousness of being observed by others is lessened in darkness. Ohio inmate Gunaratna Sarika, whose institution functions with large dorms, says he has to think of his practice as "stolen moments": "Here everybody is in each other's face. You've got to remember that almost all prisons in America were built to hold half the number of people who are in them now. I set my alarm for three or four in the morning because that's when it's the most quiet. Even though there's lights out at ten, there's guys still making noise till one or two in the morning. I look at practice as stolen moments. Sometimes I practice when I'm standing in a line, or any other time in the day when there's an opportunity."[11] In his correspondence with prisoners, Aitken Roshi often advised wetting small pieces of paper to make into earplugs. Sometimes this helps, but noise and external distractions are always going to be an element of practice.

Sitting at San Francisco Zen Center, students often have to deal with the boom boxes and loud car radios that pass by on the streets outside—plus the city sirens and the banging of early-morning garbage trucks. In the old Berkeley Zen Center, in the 1970s, the residential neighborhood was nicely quiet in the mornings, except for some cats, who always seemed to choose zazen time to do their mating outside the zendo. Their screaming seemed endless some mornings and produced not a few giggle attacks in the Zen students trying to count their breaths inside the building. There are always noise challenges.

But it would be a rare practice center that could ever duplicate the relentless and confusing sounds of banging, clanging, shouting, public address system barking, swearing, moaning, scuffle-shuffle-clank, and metallic echoes of the average prison sound environment. Still, these are also the sounds of the world, just like a city siren or the ecstasy/pain cries of a love-possessed cat. So, wherever you practice, there will be noise outside, but there is almost always more noise inside a prison.

There is also noise inside your head. This noise is part of the raw material that goes into a thorough meditation practice. And this mental noise is not particularly different whether you are practicing inside or out. Every person who meditates must face this internal noise. This is the "monkey mind" moving from one thought to another, spinning away mental energy and defying attempts at concentration. Just try some small meditation experiments and you will quickly be introduced to monkey mind.

MEDITATION TWO: BREATH COUNTING

Take five minutes. Sit up straight, on the bed, chair, or zafu; lower your eyelids but don't close them. Control your breathing from your abdomen (as opposed to your upper chest) and begin to count your exhalations from one to ten. When you get to ten, start over at one. If you loose track of the counting, don't get upset, just start over at one. Keep this up for five minutes.

How many times did you make it to ten? Did you ever get that far? How many times did you have to go back to one because you lost count?

What were the thoughts that derailed your counting? Monkey mind is the raw material of meditation. This is actually how we spend most of our mental time, swinging from branch to branch on the trees of thought. Some of these trees are fun, some are ugly, some are poison; but whatever they might be, they are also the mind's way of keeping us from the full experience of ourselves in the present moment.

Here are some more-detailed instructions: When sitting, keep your ears in line with your shoulders and your nose in line with your navel. Keep your mouth closed with your tongue on the roof of your mouth. Breathe through your nose, but control the breath from the middle of your body—from your belly, not from your chest. The top of your head should seem as if a string were holding it from above; your shoulders should remain relaxed, as if hanging down from the skeleton of skull and neck. Your spine should be slightly curved at its base, in order to point the butt more behind you than the line of your backbone.

MEDITATION THREE: KEEPING STILL

Using these detailed instructions, try sitting again for ten minutes. Keep up your one-to-ten counting, but also stay aware of your posture. Notice how often you have the impulse to move, to scratch, or to wiggle. Don't. Pay attention to keeping your eyes almost closed. When you notice they've closed all the way, you may also notice that your head is drooping. Open your eyes, straighten up, settle back again into not moving and counting your breaths. If you lose track of the numbers, don't get upset, just start over at one.

Neurological studies of meditators show that it takes between eleven and fourteen minutes for brain-wave patterns to change into the "alpha," or meditative, state. So your initial ten-minute experiments are just your training wheels, just practice for the practice. But you may not at first be able to sit still for ten minutes. So if you can't, go back to five minutes. I agree with my former teacher, Robert Aitken Roshi, that twenty-five minutes seems to be an ideal length of time for a period of sitting meditation. It gets you past that initial eleven- to fourteen-minute settling-down time, yet the session finishes before your legs have had a chance to fall completely asleep. Practitioners in some traditions sit for forty minutes or longer—and you can gradually accustom yourself to longer times if need be—but for most westerners, the twenty-five-minute period seems ideal.

Legs are a big problem. In the early decades of Buddhism in America, many gung-ho students ruined their knees, pulled tendons, or broke bones by falling (because they tried to stand up while their legs were still asleep). None of this is necessary. If your legs fall asleep twenty minutes into sitting, that's okay, you'll be up soon. But don't stand up in a hurry if your legs have fallen asleep. Even if you are in a group setting and everyone else is standing up already, don't try to stand if you can't feel your feet yet. Also, when finishing sitting in lotus or half-lotus position, hold your knees in your hands as you unfold your legs and unbend slowly.

If you are unable to sit cross-legged because of too much pain or poor circulation, use the *seiza*, or kneeling, position. Everyone in a sangha in one New York prison, where cushions are not allowed, uses seiza benches constructed by the inmates themselves; so everyone who sits there sits in the kneeling posture. This may not be the perfect position, but it does very effectively support an erect posture, even though the legs are not crossed. You can also start by using a regular chair or bench if you need to. Sometimes the old wooden pews found in some prison chapels are perfect for sitting still. No fancy equipment is necessary—work with what you have. If you can't sit in the full-lotus or half-lotus positions and want to progress to that point, start some leg stretching exercises. Experiment. You will find your way.

MEDITATION FOUR: PAST, PRESENT, FUTURE

Now try to sit for fifteen minutes. Keep up the one-to-ten count while trying to maintain proper posture. As you get distracted and lose count (which you will), notice what time the thoughts were in that distracted you. Were they thoughts about the past? Were they about the future? Just notice how often your thoughts take you out of the present moment. Meditation is about the full experience of the present moment—something that rarely happens in ordinary consciousness.

How did your legs feel after fifteen minutes? How many times did you scratch or wiggle? How often did your thoughts of past or future derail your breath counting? Probably a lot. That's okay. That's why this is called practice.

Try gradually extending the time you spend sitting still until you can successfully do a full twenty-five-minute period. Not just during meditation, but also throughout the rest of your day, notice how often your thoughts are concerned with the past or the future. Just notice. You don't have to change anything now.

As you continue experimenting with meditation techniques, consult the following list for some more things to keep in mind while setting up your own Buddhist-style meditation practice in prison.

THINGS TO KEEP IN MIND ABOUT BUDDHIST MEDITATION

1. Sitting meditation will be of little benefit if done only once in a while. For the practice to work as intended, it must be part of your everyday life. Find somewhere in your daily schedule to put your practice.

2. Don't use your inner experiences while meditating as a topic for conversation with others. Your experiences should be brought up individually with a teacher or meditation instructor, or they can be discussed in a formal class or guided discussion with other Buddhist inmates. This guideline has a long history in Bud-

dhism and is designed to prevent egocentric bragging or complaining.

3. Don't compare your inside to others' outside. Don't think, in other words, that others are better or worse at meditation than you are. Also, don't compare your own practice now to how it was yesterday or to how you hope it will be some other time. Focus on sitting right now.

4. Buddhism is not a missionary religion. Your own initial enthusiasm might lead you to want others to start meditating too. But don't bother them with your suggestions unless asked. Never put down another religion—each one has a rich tradition that we can all learn from.

5. You can do sitting meditation whether or not you consider yourself Buddhist—many Catholic monasteries, for instance, use contemplative techniques as part of their life of prayer. Islam, Judaism and Native American religions all have long and sophisticated traditions of meditative practice. You can learn from them as well.

6. Don't become preoccupied with gaining "enlightenment." You already have it—you just haven't noticed yet. So don't worry. Meditation practice is not a train that runs from point A to point B. There is no station called Enlightenment where you get off the train. Meditation is a lifetime practice of gradual opening to the truth of the world. The historical Buddha and many of the old masters did their most intensive sitting practice *after their first enlightenment experiences.*

7. It may be that you find yourself unable to sit still and concentrate for even five minutes. If this is the case, switch to walking

meditation, which is explained in the next section, but keep experimenting with short periods of sitting. People, including inmates, with attention deficit disorder/hyperactivity (ADD/H) will sometimes experience this problem. Be patient with yourself.

8. If you find yourself with recurring negative thoughts—about yourself or about other people—work with some of the vipassana-style meditation exercises. I discuss this issue in chapter 5 and give some insight meditation exercises there to try. When you have worked through these you can return to the more formless meditation styles, such as breath counting. These exercises are outlined more fully by meditation teacher Sharon Salzberg in her book, *Loving-Kindness.*

9. If you have a diagnosis of schizophrenia—or another serious, persistent disorder—you should not do sitting meditation unless you are keeping up a medication regime that controls your symptoms. Check with medical staff, and a meditation instructor, before starting your practice.

Another meditation technique, from the Tibetan tradition, involves mental visualizations. Calming, breath-based meditation is always recommended before attempting visualizations, so practice in the techniques described so far is always important. Visualizations are meant to be done when the mind is at rest. The images are not meant to be experienced through the eyes but, rather, mentally, through the mind's eye. Kathleen McDonald's book, *How to Meditate: A Practical Guide,* is an excellent guide to beginning this technique. The following is her advice for an initial meditation exercise to try.

MEDITATION FIVE: THE BODY OF LIGHT

Sit comfortably, with your back straight, and breathe naturally. When your mind is calm and clear, visualize in the space above your head a sphere of white light, somewhat smaller than the size of your head, pure, transparent and formless. Spend several minutes concentrating on the presence of the light. Don't worry if it does not appear sharply; it is enough just to feel it is there. Contemplate that the sphere of light represents all universal goodness, love and wisdom: the fulfillment of your own highest potential. Then visualize that it decreases in size until it is about one inch in diameter and descends through the top of your head to your heart-center. From there it begins to expand once more, slowly spreading to fill your entire body. As it does, all the solid parts of your body dissolve and become light—your organs, bones, blood vessels, tissue and skin all become pure, formless white light.

Concentrate on the experience of your body as a body of light. Think that all problems, negativities, and hindrances have completely vanished, and that you have reached a state of wholeness and perfection. Feel serene and joyful. If any thought or distracting object should appear in your mind, let is also dissolve into white light. Meditate in this way for as long as you can.[12]

Because of differences in personality and sensory organization, some people respond better to visualization techniques that to other, more formless meditation styles. If you are just starting, you should give this technique a try. Each Tibetan tradition has its own curriculum of progressively more complicated visualization exercises.

These step-by-step meditations are also similar to the word-based *koan* curricula used in some Zen lineages. Koans are traditional Zen stories which are used as the object (or subject) of meditation. Robert Aitken Roshi describes them as presentations of the universal through the particular. Here is a sample koan from Yün-men, a tenth-century Chinese teacher. Yün-men was giving a lecture to his monks in their assembly hall. He said: "All people have a light, but when they look at it they do not see it, so it is obscure. What is everyone's light?" No one replied, so the master himself said, on their behalf, "The communal hall, the Buddha shrine, the kitchen pantry, the mountain gate." [13]

While you meditate, you can hold Yün-men's question in mind: "What is everyone's light?" Or you could focus on his poetic, yet matter-of-fact, answer to his own question: "The communal hall, the Buddha shrine, the kitchen pantry, the mountain gate." What is he saying? What do you say? That is the work of the koan.

WALKING THE WALK

Musô Soseki, a fourteenth-century Japanese poet and Zen teacher, once told his students, "An ancient master said, 'The mountains, the rivers, the whole earth, the entire array of phenomena are all oneself.' If you can absorb the essence of this message, there are no activities outside of meditation: you dress in meditation and eat in meditation; you walk, stand, sit, and lie down in meditation; you perceive and cognize in meditation; you experience joy, anger, sadness, and happiness in meditation."[14]

For prison practice, maybe we could change the old master's words to something like: "The cement, the bars, the urinals, the yells in the night, the entire array of phenomena are all oneself." It's true. Old Musô is talking about the Buddhist concept of mindfulness, stressed by teachers like Thich Nhat Hanh, Henepola Gunaratana, and Shunryu Suzuki—among many others. *Mindfulness* means bringing the attentive mind of meditation to all daily activities. It means retaining a mental stillness while in physical motion, to achieve what Christian, Islamic, and Jewish mystics have called "continual prayer," or, sometimes, "living in the presence of God." Some Native Americans mean the same thing when they talk about "the God of the Close and the Near." In this mindful state, every daily action becomes sacred, each word or gesture becomes a prayer.

But mindfulness does not mean thinking some kind of sacred thoughts while doing other things. It means just doing the thing: looking up a word in the dictionary, sweeping out a room, scraping tasteless food off a metal tray. Perhaps the easiest way to begin the practice of mindfulness is by trying walking meditation. Walking meditation is often done in the meditation hall between periods of sitting meditation. It helps wake up the legs and the mind before returning to the cushion.

In the Japanese Zen tradition, structured, group walking meditation is called *kinhin*. The walking is meant to be done "mindfully"—that is, with attention—while still continuing the same breath counting or other meditation technique that you do while seated. It is not just an extension of zazen; it is itself a moving zazen. If you have the opportunity to do walking meditation as a group in the meditation hall, your pace should be the same as that of everyone else. It then becomes an exercise in blending your practice with the practice of others. You should keep about the same distance from the person in front of you throughout the walking. Posture is still important: your back should still be straight, eyes cast in front of you at about forty-five degrees; hands should be in whatever position your local instructor advises. In most traditions this position is either the left or right hand balled around the bent thumb with the opposite hand covering; the hands are then held at a level one fist above the navel, with the elbows out to the sides.

Walking meditation can be done solo in prison in a variety of ways. Try timing your steps to fit with the pace of your inhalations and exhalations. In this way, even walking at a normal pace can become practice. Count how many steps you take while exhaling, then while inhaling. Usually the exhale is longer, maybe three steps, compared to only two for the inhale. Experiment. Find your own pace and your own way of walking mindfully.

When walking outside, you can count exhales on a *mala*, the 108-bead Buddhist rosary. In a prison environment, walking meditation is often done in the yard, the outside exercise area. This means that the self-consciousness produced by walking in a seemingly odd but attentive manner may sometimes become such a distraction that mindfulness is replaced by embarrassment. And territory is often quite clearly staked out in yard situations, so it may take a prison sangha some time to establish a walking area unhindered by the territorial demands of inmate factions. But it has been done, and nonpracticing inmates can often learn to respect the practice, even if they don't understand it.

Sitting Inside

Walking meditation doesn't have to be done outdoors. Pacing in the cell is an ancient prison tradition, and it takes only a small mental shift to turn that mindless pacing into pacing practice. Try the next meditation.

MEDITATION SIX: PACING

Do you already know how many paces from one wall to the other? You have probably counted them already. But how is it that you paced before? Like a madman—crazy and distracted and caged? If so, try it differently. Slow down your pace and attend to your breathing as you walk. Keep your breathing controlled from the abdomen and notice the feel of one foot lifting, moving up and forward, coming down, connecting with the floor. Notice the shifting of the weight, the lifting of the other foot. Do all this slowly, attentively. Try to do it for a full ten minutes. Let everything around you—the sights and sounds and smells—be swept up into your simple, focused walking.

Whatever form walking meditation takes, it is still sitting; that is, it should continue to be the practice of stilling the mind, dwelling peacefully in the present moment, even though the body is in motion. Walking meditation is often very helpful if you experience extremes of emotion or mental distractions that are so strong that you are prevented from settling into your usual seated meditation. Buddhist teacher Thich Nhat Hanh prescribes walking meditation especially during times of anger. In his book *Peace Is Every Step,* he recommends walking when anger arises, noticing the breath and using the following mental formula:

> *Breathing in, I know that anger is here.*
> *Breathing out, I know that the anger is me.*
> *Breathing in, I know that anger is unpleasant.*
> *Breathing out, I know this feeling will pass.*
> *Breathing in, I am calm.*
> *Breathing out, I am strong enough to take care of this anger.*

He explains further: "To lessen the unpleasant feeling brought about by the anger, we give our whole heart and mind to the practice of walking meditation, combining our breath with our steps and giving full attention to the contact between the soles of our feet and the earth. As we walk, we recite this verse, and wait until we are calm enough to look directly at the anger. Until then, we can enjoy our breathing, our walking, and the beauties of our environment. After awhile, our anger will subside and we will feel stronger. Then we can begin to observe the anger directly and try to understand it."[15]

OTHER PRACTICES

Bowing and prostrations are a common part of most Buddhist traditions. Learning to bow is often difficult for Americans, who equate it with Old Testament warnings about not worshipping (bowing down before) idols or "graven images." From an Asian cultural perspective, bowing is just a form of greeting. Deeper bows and full prostrations are seen from a Buddhist religious perspective as acts that empty the ego, not as the worship of some external idol.

Although we often have images of the Buddha in our meditation halls, it is important to remember that for the first several hundred years of Buddhist history no images were used at all. Sometimes just the outline of a hand or footprint was all that was used to remind people of the historical Buddha. Sculptural figures began to be made by Buddhists influenced by Greek culture brought east by Alexander the Great.

Whatever the reasons, bowing is often problematic for westerners. Try it anyway, despite your reservations. Don't just nod your head. A proper bow does not involve bending the neck; it should be controlled from the waist. At the very least, you can start by bowing to your cushion, bench, or chair before beginning a period of sitting meditation. This simple act comes from a long tradition of reverence for the earthly ground on which we sit—and out of which our practice must emerge. It is also a formal gesture that marks the beginning and ending of a special part of the day, a time different in quality from the rest of the day. The proper way to do bows and prostrations, especially in the meditation hall, differs from one tradition to another, so if an outside dharma center is helping you inside, follow the guidance of that tradition.

The full prostration—which involves going down to the floor or ground and touching it with forehead, arms, and legs—is also a practice that may be found across a wide variety of Buddhist traditions. Again, the exact physical form may differ slightly from tradition to tradition, but the practice is virtually universal in Buddhist cultures. I once attended a seven-day retreat with a Korean Zen master who had his students do 108 prostrations each morning before sitting meditation. It was an aerobic awakening.

Chanting or recitation is another practice you might want to try. It is a way of experiencing Buddhist teachings in a different sensory mode than silent reading provides. Chanting is similar to hearing a poet read a poem aloud, compared to reading the same poem in a book. Like meditation, using the voice to sound out the text, syllable by syllable, requires a very focused form of attention. (One Vietnamese abbot, who runs a monastery in the United States, tells his monks to bring their chanting speed up to such a pace that the slightest distracting thought will derail their flow of words.) Try vocalizing the text you choose in a monotone and keep a comfortable but challenging pace by tapping a finger on something solid. In a Zen temple, this beat is kept by a wooden drum carved to look like a fish, called a *mokugyo* in Japanese. You are unlikely to have one in prison, so use whatever is at hand for percussion.

Again, each Buddhist tradition has slightly different ways of chanting and different choices of texts for their services and recitations. The *Heart Sutra* is recited in many traditions of Buddhism, so it might be a good text to start with. Another translation, used in the Honolulu Diamond Sangha, a lay Zen center where I practice, goes like this:

Avalokiteshvara Bodhisattva, practicing deep Prajna Paramita,
clearly saw that all five skandhas are empty,
transforming anguish and distress.
Shariputra, form is no other than emptiness,
emptiness no other than form;
form is exactly emptiness, emptiness exactly form;
sensation, perception, formulation, consciousness are also like this.
Shariputra, all things are essentially empty—not born, not destroyed;
not stained, not pure; without loss, without gain.
Therefore in emptiness there is no form, no sensation,
perception, formulation, consciousness;
no eye, ear, nose, tongue, body, mind,
no color, sound, scent, taste, touch, thought;
no seeing and so on to no thinking;
no ignorance and also no ending of ignorance,
and so on to no old age and death,
and also no ending of old age and death;
no anguish, cause of anguish, cessation, path;
no wisdom and no attainment. Since there is nothing to attain,
the Bodhisattva lives by Prajna Paramita, with no hindrance in the
mind; no hindrance and therefore no fear;
far beyond delusive thinking, right here is nirvana.
All Buddhas of past, present, and future live by Prajna Paramita
attaining Anuttara-samyak-sambodhi.
Therefore know that Prajna Paramita
is the great sacred mantra, the great vivid mantra,
the unsurpassed mantra, the supreme mantra,
which completely removes all anguish.
This is truth not mere formality.
Therefore set forth the Prajna Paramita mantra,
set forth this mantra and proclaim:
Gate gate paragate parasamgate
Bodhi svaha!

Sitting Inside

There are literally thousands of commentaries attempting to explain this, one of the shortest of all Buddhist sutras, so don't worry if you can't understand it. Suffice it to say for now that this recitation reminds us of the interplay of emptiness and form that is at the heart of Buddhist realization. *Emptiness* is an important Buddhist concept, but don't think that it means just "nothing," or some sort of spatial vacuum that physicists would study. Emptiness means that our world is not as solid as our habitual experience leads us to believe. It is a way of saying that nouns may also be seen as verbs and that particles may also be waves. For example, the experience you think of as "fear," is (from a Buddhist point of view) just a passing intersection of tendencies that will evaporate. This being you call your self—and have named Julie or Frank or Raul—is also just a process that will quickly pass away. Every "thing" you can name is really a process as evanescent as a soap bubble.

The *Heart Sutra* restates and emphasizes one of the most important discoveries of the Buddha: there is "no abiding self." The repeated recitation of this sutra can begin the process of teaching you what that means. You will begin to notice key phrases, such as "right here is nirvana," and you will want to figure them out.

Many longer sutras are now available in English translation. If you have access to these, you could start with any of these and chant them in a monotone, at a pace tapped out by one hand as you chant. You should keep the speed fast enough so that you have no opportunity to think any other thoughts—all you can do is vocalize the words as your eyes move along the pages. For hundreds of years the sutras were kept only in memory and recited as needed. They come down to us from an oral tradition, and, like the Koran of Islam or the psalms of the Jewish and Christian sacred books, they are best experienced as recitations rather than as silent readings.

If an outside dharma center is helping your institution, follow the guidance and translations they provide for morning, evening, and mealtime chants.

REFUGE AND PRECEPTS

An easy daily recitation would be the "three refuges," which is an ancient and basic invocation common to all forms of Buddhism. It is a reminder of the "three treasures" that support our practice: the historical *Buddha* (plus all those who have awakened before and since his time); the *dharma* (the teaching, or method of practice); and the *sangha* (community of other beings practicing Buddhism). The idea is that our lives are given shelter and safety by committing ourselves to the long line of awakened beings, to their teachings, and to the community we practice with. You can recite these three refuges, at the same time, each day:

> *I take refuge in the Buddha,*
> *I take refuge in the dharma,*
> *I take refuge in the sangha.*

If you want to, you can bring your hands together and bow once for each of the refuges.

Another recitation that many traditions consider important is that of the five lay precepts, which are the vows a layperson takes during a refuge ceremony. This ceremony is like baptism in the Christian tradition in that it is a public declaration that you are Buddhist and you commit yourself to these guidelines for behavior. Other traditions use what are called the ten grave precepts and recommend that their students gather on a regular basis to recite these precepts together. Some teachers prefer to call the precepts "trainings."

I'll discuss the implications of these precepts/trainings for behavior in prisons in greater detail in chapter 4. For now, please read my version on the next page, of these vows or trainings. They should become the extension and the context of your sitting still. Recite them as often as you can.

THE TEN GRAVE PRECEPTS

1. I take up the path of not killing and of encouraging and protecting life.
2. I take up the path of generosity and of not taking what is not given.
3. I take up the path of not misusing sexuality.
4. I take up the path of not lying and of truthful communication.
5. I take up the path of not intoxicating myself or others.
6. I take up the path of gentle speech and of not speaking ill of others.
7. I take up the path of not praising self and disparaging others.
8. I take up the path of not being possessive with the dharma.
9. I take up the path of loving-kindness and of not indulging in anger.
10. I take up the path of not abusing the three treasures: the Buddha, the dharma and the sangha.

CHAPTER 2 NOTES

1. John Daido Loori, "Lotus in the Fire: Prison, Practice, and Freedom," typescript, n.d.
2. Fleet Maull, "Prison Monasticism," *Turning Wheel*, winter 1992, 21. The charnel field meditation mentioned here was an early Buddhist practice of doing meditation near decaying bodies to help sangha members remember their final end.
3. Kerry J. Greenwell, personal communication, 1997.
4. Lama Yontan Gonpa, personal communication, 1997.
5. Greenwell.
6. Jarvis Masters, "Pipe-Down Dharma," *The Mindfulness Bell*, May-Aug. 1997, 9.
7. Paul Dewey, personal communication, 1997.
8. Eihei Dôgen, "A Generally Recommended Mode of Sitting Meditation," in *Minding Mind: A Course in Basic Meditation,* trans. Thomas Cleary, (Boston: Shambhala Publications, 1995), 25.
9. Foxin Bencai, "Guidelines for Sitting Meditation," in *Minding Mind,* 20-21.
10. Herbert Benson, *The Relaxation Response,* (New York: Avon Books), 1975.
11. Gunaratna Sarika, personal communication, 1997.
12. Kathleen McDonald, *How to Meditate: A Practical Guide* (Boston: Wisdom Publications, 1984), 114.
13. Ejo, "Absorption in the Treasury of Light," in *Minding Mind,* 59.
14. Musô Soseki, in *Roaring Stream: A New Zen Reader,* ed. Nelson Foster and Jack Shoemaker (Hopewell, N.J.: Ecco Press, 1996), 243.
15. Thich Nhat Hanh, *Peace Is Every Step: The Path of Mindfulness in Everyday Life* (New York: Bantam Books, 1992), 61.

The Practice of Power

"If one speaks or acts with a pure mind, happiness will follow, like a shadow that never leaves." —Dhammapada

Prisons are places where power, real or imagined, is the currency of exchange. As institutions, prisons are meant to deprive their residents of as much power as possible. Simple freedoms that people on the outside take for granted—like the ability to associate with whom you wish, to travel, to write letters, to shop, to choose your own food and clothing, to make your own schedule, to be alone—all these rights or possibilities are removed by the very act of incarceration.

To enter a prison is to be stripped (often literally, as a kind of degradation ceremony) of personal power and individual choice. This stripping makes the drive for power even more urgent to the prisoner, who is left without any of the most basic ways of being a healthy human being.

Prison administrators think they have power, and they try to hold onto it. Prison guards think they have power, and they, too, attempt to protect themselves and to reap the benefits of the few powers they enjoy. Penal institutions also allow (even encourage) prisoners, if they wish, to compete for power with each other. By a ten-to-one ratio, prison populations are predominantly male. Sheer overcrowding, plus our culturally programmed male aggressiveness, combine to intensify the power issues that pervade prison life.

THE POWER OF HARASSMENT

The games of competition and ego-enhancement inside prisons can also entrap people from outside who want to be involved in prison work. The world of prisons is a "closed system," in the sense that systems analysts speak of such things. As the weakest point of any closed system is the place where it interfaces with another system—in this case, the outside world—the games of power are often expressed by guards and prison administrators toward those who want access to inmates: prisoners' families, twelve-step fellowships, legal assistance groups, as well as journalists and religious organizations. Hawaii's Oahu Central Correctional Facility, for example, used to have a guard at the gate to the visitors' parking lot asking each family to show a copy of current auto insurance. This was a petty harassment that, as usual, hit the poor the hardest—because prisoners' families tend to be poor and are, therefore, more likely to have no auto insurance. No other parking lot in the state requires such documentation.

These power games are not usually overtly aggressive. Passive aggression, a game played by government functionaries worldwide, is the predominant style. In the Oahu example, for instance, visitors were not turned away at gunpoint but rather by an overly meticulous adherence to regulations. Passive aggressive techniques of institutional power also include "forgetting" to do things, losing important paperwork, making visitors wait protracted lengths of time, and a dramatic, but hypocritical, concern for the safety of inmates or visitors.

U.S. dharma groups have often been subjected to these peevish power plays by prison authorities. The following account, from Gunaratna Sarika, the Buddhist inmate from Ohio, is typical:

> The previous chaplain did not want our group here at all. On one occasion, he sort of went off the deep end and called us all Satanists, idol-worshipers, and a few other things. But we survived. Sometimes our meetings were cancelled without prior notice or without a rea-

son. For a time the administration would not work
with our outside volunteers as far as scheduling goes.
The prison would say, "You can have Friday afternoons,"
even though the volunteer had made it clear that he was
not available for that time. Then, when our volunteer
does make the time by rearranging his personal schedule, the prison would change the time and/or day on
which we were supposed to meet. This still occasionally
happens but not as much as it used to. I think that most
of the prison staff has come to accept that we are serious about what we are doing and also, by talking together, they are coming to understand more about what
Buddhism really represents. We now have two new chaplains and they help us out as much as the administration allows. They have given the Buddhist group a lot
of respect and I think they deserve credit for that.[1]

Rev. Shu Ho (Mike Bonasso) of Cloud Water Zendo in Cleveland,
Ohio, began working with inmates at the Marion facility in the summer
of 1996. After many attempts to meet as a group, Sarika, the inmate who
had originally asked for Shu Ho's help, filed a suit against the prison
administration that had blocked inmate access to Buddhist teachers. After the warden and the Seventh Day Adventist chaplain were called by
the pro bono attorney to give depositions in the suit, the two administrators issued an internal directive prohibiting any Buddhist prisoners from
meeting in the same room—an obvious and petty retaliation for their
legal inconvenience.

Kobutsu Kevin Malone, a Zen monk who has worked for years with
prisoners in the state of New York, describes his first experience visiting
Sing Sing Prison in 1991. "I remember waiting two and a half hours to
get my photo taken. It was actually kind of degrading," he says. More
passive aggression. After he gained access to the prisoners, Kobutsu says,
the power games continued. Instead of allowing them to meet in the
chapel or a classroom, the Sing Sing administration assigned the dharma

group to meet in a storage room.

> We were sitting in a kind of general storage room in the
> hospital building. It was filthy. I got donations for
> some zafus, but the administration said they were not
> "articles of worship" so we could not bring them inside.
> They would not recognize us as a religious group. Fi-
> nally, we got an attorney and after a couple of letters
> they [the prison administration] recognized us as a reli-
> gious group. Gradually we got stuff inside. The *kyôsaku*
> [2] stick really freaked them out. Here is this 250-pound
> Irishman who is going to be hitting their babies. But
> they got over it. We now have a kind of traveling zendo
> which is kept in a locker. Everything we need is inside.[3]

Examples of such deliberate sabotage of Buddhist groups trying to
work inside could fill another whole book. Versions of this kind of ob-
struction have been repeated, over and over, from one institution to another throughout the country.

RELIGIOUS POWER PLAYS

There seem to be two main reasons for such overt hostility toward Buddhist groups in prisons. One is pure religious prejudice—the kind of
ignorance that leads to the use of such words as "idol-worshipping,"
"cult," and "Satanism." (It is amusing to remember some pundit's defi-
nition of "cult" as any religion that's not big enough to have a university
and a football team.) Sadly, it is sometimes the Christian chaplains who
are most at fault for promoting such ignorance and (un-Christian) spite-
fulness.

Despite the increasing popularity of Buddhism in the United States,
mentioning it may still set off images of the occult in the minds of some
Americans. Reverend Kusala Ratnakaruna, a monk who has worked with
both adult and juvenile prisoners in the Los Angeles area, recounts the
reaction of a guard at Lancaster State Prison when he first began his

visits. The guard asked what he was there for and Kusala explained he was a Buddhist volunteer. The guard just shook his head and said, "Oh great! Pretty soon they'll have astrologers coming inside." [4]

The second reason for negative reactions to Buddhist groups inside would seem rather humorous were it not so prevalent—namely, the belief of some security and administrative personnel that zazen, chanting, and other meditation practices are part of, or will lead to, martial arts training. John Daido Loori elaborates, based on his first experiences in Greenhaven Correctional Facility in New York.

> Initially, we had some difficulty creating the sitting group simply because the guards didn't know us. They knew the Protestant minister, they knew the Catholic priest, they knew the Jewish rabbi and they knew the Islamic imam, but they had no idea who the Zen Buddhists were. All they knew was that we were somehow vaguely connected with kung fu, and they certainly did not want martial arts being taught to prisoners. Consequently, the guards made it difficult to gain entry. There was always some kind of red tape. A two or three-hour car ride to the prison would result in having to spend most of our time in the waiting room, with hardly a chance to see the inmates. [5]

Staff suspicions about martial arts are always best addressed directly by prison dharma workers. Time taken to explain what is going on to guards and chaplaincy staff is never wasted, even if suspicions persist for awhile. It is much simpler to actively rule out the martial arts fear right away. Even so, an inmate in an Ohio state prison described how nervous the guards became the first few times their group sat together in total silence. It was such uncommon behavior inside that they were very suspicious and interpreted it as the calm before some dreadful storm.

Joan Halifax reminds us that security staff have needs also. "They are in prison too," she says, "and it sometimes seems to them that prisoners get more attention, more services, or more sympathy from outsiders than they do." They may have a point, yet it is my experience that custodial staff will not attend classes or other functions together with prisoners. Although some dharma groups have talked about this, I don't know of any that have succeeded in setting up meditation programs for guards.

Although prison administrators may possess certain real powers, like choosing what food to buy or deciding the visiting days and hours, the real sum of the power equation in prisons is determined by the subtle algebra of guard and inmate economic transactions. The factions and personalities of these two forces assure a continuing, dynamic interaction between the two camps that resembles the formalities of war—with spies, stormtroops, generals, privates, and propagandists on each side.

INMATE POWER PLAYS

Administrators and guards are not the only ones, by any means, who play with power inside. Dharma groups must face the power issues among the inmates themselves. Kobutsu Malone, for one, encountered fierce internal power struggles among the prisoners who were in his first group at Sing Sing.

> The guys I originally met had everything planned about what was going to happen. The group was started by some other people with the idea of stress reduction. I went in with them two or three times. But the meditation was only about ten minutes, the rest of the time they just spent bull-shitting. My first time alone with the inmates, they said they wanted to have a business meeting and started doing flow-charts. They wanted me to set up outside corporations. I had been warned about this in the orientation and I can smell a con a mile away. I just told them, "I'm not here to run an organization or be a front for your needs. From here on

out, we will meet for ten minutes *after* we've done two hours of zazen." Some of them got really pissed off and attempted to force me out. I had to tell them, "I'm running the program." One of them attempted to forge some papers with volunteer signatures. We sat half hour periods. They didn't like it. Finally, I ended up with three men—none of them part of the original group. [6]

So it is possible that Buddha, dharma, and sangha—the three treasures of Buddhism—can themselves become involved in the power game. Geoffrey Shugen Arnold, the prison dharma coordinator for New York's Zen Mountain Monastery, explains: "In a prison situation, there are great struggles with the environment that you don't have in other practice situations. It is an environment with a total lack of trust and in which positioning for power is the main order of business. We have decided against any form of ordination within the prisons. It would be a powderkeg. There are prisoners with such charisma, with such social skills that they have the potential to take practice groups in a whole different direction to suit their own power needs." [7]

Other Buddhist organizations make other decisions about the ordination of prisoners. Some groups will perform refuge ceremonies, which usually include the five lay vows or trainings. Sometimes called "lay ordination," refuge ceremonies (as mentioned in chapter 2) are really more akin to the Christian sacrament of baptism, in that they define the participant as a Buddhist. Also, as in baptism, a new name is often given to the initiate to signify a change of identity. Some sanghas will also give full monastic ordinations to certain inmates. In 1997, Tetsugen Bernard Glassman, a Zen roshi and social activist, ordained Fleet Maull, who at the time was an inmate in a federal prison.

Buddhism comes to the United States from patriarchal and Confucian cultures where there are definite distinctions in hierarchy between monks and abbots, men and women, laypeople and clerics. This tendency is still alive in the bestowal of titles and in the not-so-subtle color differences of robes. In some Japanese traditions, for instance, a blue *rakusu* [8] is lower than a black rakusu—and a brown one is better than either. These kinds of status distinctions can be toxic in regular sanghas and can be even more lethal inside the power-vigilant world of prison society. It will be a challenge for dharma practitioners both inside and outside to figure out this power koan as Buddhism continues to develop in America.

Dharma prison workers must also be aware of their own personal power needs, which might be expressed even in their desire to work with the powerless in prison—an automatic one-up situation, in which the prison volunteer is almost always richer, more free, better educated, and (perhaps) more spiritually skilled than the inmate Buddhist.

Prisons provide, quite literally, a captive audience for religious workers. There is sometimes a form of economic/emotional exchange whereby prisoners demonstrate change of heart so religious workers can feel good about their work. By impressing religious workers, inmates are sometimes cultivating advocates for early release or errand people to get things done on the outside. Some religious groups are allowed to provide food, clothing, or other personal items to inmates. In such cases, they can draw an inmate crowd to their services, creating a congregation intent on getting these small material benefits. Sometimes inmates feel that they can reduce their time by participating in religious activities and by demonstrating all the symptoms of religious conversion. This "jailhouse religion" phenomenon is familiar to parole boards and prison chaplains around the country—and should be realistically kept in mind by dharma volunteers working inside.

THE POWER OF LAW

Sometimes, when prison administrations are especially stubborn, the game of power must be taken to the courts. This situation can come about in several ways. Geoffrey Shugen Arnold talks about his sangha's early dealings with the prison system in New York.

It was in the early 1980s that we received a letter from several inmates in the Greenhaven facility in upstate New York, expressing interest in Zen practice. Initially, John Daido Loori and the other volunteers had difficulty gaining access to the prison—the gate clearance could not be found, escorts would be late. Eventually, the inmates initiated a class action suit against the institution for obstructing their ability to practice their religious faith. The case was handled, pro bono, by a prestigious law firm in New York City, and was settled out of court. The result was that Buddhism was recognized as a bona fide religion in the New York State correctional system.

Since that time, the attitudes of the prison guards and administrators has changed dramatically, such that they can oftentimes be relied upon to help when problems do arise. Unfortunately, based on the many letters that we respond to from inmates across the country, there are still many prisons where there are big obstacles for Buddhist inmates. [9]

Since winning that original case, Zen Mountain Monastery has been asked by the state corrections department to help other New York prisons serve their Buddhist inmates. The monastery now acts in an advisory capacity to the state correctional agency in Albany and has been able to help the state improve its Volunteer Clearance System to facilitate visits to inmates by outside practitioners.

These kinds of lawsuits have paid off in similar ways in other locations. Many Buddhist groups report the establishment of very good institutional relations after what may have been years of legal and bureaucratic skirmishing. Inmates who have educated themselves to become "jailhouse lawyers" have a well-deserved reputation for legal expertise. So dharma groups often can (and should) rely on the prisoners themselves to initiate and handle freedom of religion actions against prison administrations. The sangha may fill the role of consultant, or liaison with outside legal resources. Sometimes dharma leaders will be called upon to give legal depositions or other forms of testimony to explain the nature of Buddhism and the intent of the sangha in trying to work with inmates. Arnold is happy with the results of the legal efforts in New York. "State policies always get played out in the daily details of prison procedures and the attitude has done a 180-degree turn since the lawsuit. Now it's the guards who advocate for us. Before, it was not unusual to get letters we sent to inmates returned to us in the mail with no explanation for why they weren't delivered. Now we have regular correspondence with about one hundred inmates with few hassles." [10]

As mentioned in chapter 1, the Religious Freedom Restoration Act was passed by the U.S. Congress in 1993. The RFRA was meant to increase (or restore) protected religious freedoms that had been limited by a 1990 U.S. Supreme Court decision in a case called *The Oregon Employment Division v. Smith*. In this decision, the court ruled that the "free exercise" clause of the First Amendment of the Bill of Rights does not apply to laws that are "valid, reasonable, and generally applicable."

Prior to the 1990 ruling, any governmental entity attempting to limit religious freedoms had to demonstrate some "compelling state interest" for doing so. The 1990 decision, in effect, loosened the criteria and made it easier for governments to limit religious expression. Government agencies, including prisons, could cite a "reasonable" concern, like security, to justify limiting religious expression. The RFRA was meant to remedy this situation, and in the years 1993 through 1997, state and federal prisons attempted to come to terms with the RFRA by allowing more—and more diverse—religious activities in prisons. A number of Buddhist inmates used the RFRA to win concessions from slow-to-respond administrators. A Texas RFRA case was eventually taken before the Supreme Court, in an effort to test the constitutionality of the law, and in 1997, the Court ruled that the RFRA was unconstitutional. In response, several members of Congress vowed to rewrite and repass the RFRA; the resulting Religious Liberty Protection Act (RLPA) was signed into law by President Clinton in 2000.

Without the RFRA, inmate suits had to focus on discrimination and fairness issues. In other words, if Christian inmates are allowed the use of a chapel but Moslem or Buddhist prisoners are not then there is a basis for legal remedy. Administrators often get around this fairness issue by making up arbitrary rules, such as requiring that there needs to be a certain number of inmates who are Buddhist before they can use the chapel.

SETTING ASIDE THE POWER GAME

The concept of mindfulness was introduced in chapter 2. Mindfulness particularly comes into play when inmates or outside Buddhist volunteers try to deal skillfully and patiently with abuses of power. In his book, *Mindfulness in Plain English,* Henepola Gunaratana tells us that "mindfulness is the essence of patience."[11] We see what is going on and we accept it. Please note that "accept" in this sense does not mean the same thing as "approve of." Meditation teaches us patience with ourselves, an acceptance of what Tibetan Buddhists call the "waterfall of thought" that gushes out of control through our awareness. Mindfulness lets us look outward into the world and practice patience with others—who suffer just as much, if not more, than we do.

A way Buddhist inmates have found to deal with the internal power jostling in prisons is to view the whole seemingly negative environment as an opportunity for practice. Prison Dharma Network founder Fleet Maull explains that what is important is

> accepting some responsibility for the situation you're in—not guilt, but responsibility. Then you just don't get involved in a lot of blaming—feeling persecuted, oppressed, and abused, and seeing the institution, authority, and the world as your absolute enemy. It's a challenge not to buy into that hatred, because the environment in prison is continually inviting you to do that in every possible way. That's where practice comes in, because when you get a glimpse of nonduality and egolessness, you just don't solidify things into "me against the system." Of course, anger still comes up, but there's space around all that stuff.[12]

In other words, it is possible to give up the power game through practice. And it is possible to gain responsibility—the opposite of blame—by viewing the power situation as a whole—guards and prisoners, administrators and outsiders: all are part of the same suffering, the same ignorance and greed. As long as we can view others as other, we seem to be allowed to hate them. When practice gives us the insight that we're all in the same leaky boat, our blaming becomes uncomfortable and our power plays seem petty. Kerry Greenwell, from Indiana State Prison, elaborates:

> Our barriers and difficulties are usually caused by administration and/or guards. And this is caused by the usual misconceptions that people who aren't informed have about Buddhism in general. There is some religious prejudice from a couple of the higher-ups. In the beginning, through our own ignorance, we used to fight with them on a regular basis. I've found that if we use patience with a bit of wisdom we can usually get things done. After all, these people are suffering from the same samsaric [cause and effect] principles as we are. All this has become an opportunity for me to practice the virtues of compassion, loving-kindness, patience, etc. [13]

Another example comes from Frankie Parker, who before beginning the practice of Buddhism was a violent and rebellious inmate in the Arkansas state prison system. He was known for beating up other inmates and cursing at the guards. In about 1990, he was thrown into solitary ("the hole") for the umpteenth time, and he angrily demanded that the guard give him a copy of the Bible—the one book allowed even to prisoners in solitary. "Here's your Bible!" the guard shouted back and threw a copy of the *Dhammapada* (an ancient Buddhist text) into Parker's cell. This was another abuse of power, an ironic game in which the guard had apparently won another round. But after the guard had gone, Parker picked up the book and read:

1. Everything has mind in the lead, has mind in the fore-front, is made by mind. If one speaks or acts with a corrupt mind, misery will follow, as the wheel of a cart follows the foot of the ox.

It must have taken him two or three readings to get the gist of the opening. The metaphor of ox and cartwheel might have at first seemed similar to biblical language. But "mind?" He continued reading:

2. Everything has mind in the lead, has mind in the fore-front, is made by mind. If one speaks or acts with a pure mind, happiness will follow, like a shadow that never leaves.

Then there came two verses that repeated themselves in the parallel construction so familiar in ancient rhetoric. But these next verses were more concrete than the previous ones and hit Frankie Parker where it hurt.

3. "He reviled me; he injured me; he defeated me; he de-prived me." In those who harbor such grudges, hatred never ceases.
4. "He reviled me; he injured me; he defeated me; he deprived me." In those who do not harbor such grudges, hatred eventually ceases.[14]

The *Dhammapada* is thought to be one of the oldest texts in Buddhism and may contain the most accurate version we have of some of the historical Buddha's original words. Unlike the many long and ornate sutras written down in later years, the *Dhammapada* is made up of brief aphorisms; as in the parables of Jesus, this brevity helps readers remember each of the seemingly simple messages.

Frankie Parker had been a very angry man, who was, quite literally, "reviled, injured, defeated, and deprived" by a power structure bent on punishing him for the very real murders he committed. But as he began to memorize some of the aphorisms, he also began to see that the power to hurt and to hate was an aspect of mind—and that there might be some way out of his habitual suffering. Gradually, Parker stopped fighting others and defying his keepers. Toward the end of his life, he was appreciated by the guards and the other inmates for his peacemaking and for the gentle quality of his daily behavior.

Thus, the abuse of power by a prison guard became the ironic teaching, the opening of a dharma gate, that would eventually lead Parker to calm his anger, to tame his blaming and his hatreds, and to die peacefully of a state-administered lethal injection. Despite the fact that he apparently lost his power game with the state—he was executed despite the efforts of many people who pleaded for clemency—he still did not really lose. Meditation practice made it possible for him to step out of the power game altogether and to accept the workings of the world.

The Buddhist strategy for dealing with abusive uses of power must always adhere to the first precept, which prohibits our doing harm to others. In other words, our tactics must be nonviolent both in deed and in thought. Nonviolence is a process. It is not a dogma with a rule book that tells us what to do in every situation. Conflicts over power come from what is seen in Buddhism as the *three poisons*—greed, hatred, and ignorance. Mindfulness helps us to see our own greed, our own rejection of others, and our own inability to understand. When we realize that others are made miserable by the same poisons, this is the beginning of compassion and nonviolence.

There is always adversity in prisons. For Buddhist inmates, at least, it is the patient and skillful use of nonviolent techniques that will constitute mindful, real-world action against injustice. Nonviolent techniques include legal methods as well as such activities as fasting, letter writing, circulating petitions, creating art and poetry, education of other inmates and of staff, and organizing family or other outside advocates. The Buddhism of compassion-in-action always tries to see the broader situation, the wider and longer-term aspects of any conflict.

In talking about kinds of practice, in chapter 2, I did not mention the *gatha*. Gathas are short poems or vows that may be recited to oneself throughout the day. Robert Aitken Roshi, in his book *The Dragon Who Never Sleeps*, explains how gathas are used and structured: The first line sets out the circumstances, the second line is the vow to change, and the last two lines follow through with the behavioral outcomes of the vow. Aitken also gives us his own gathas for life in the real world; here is one that might help in circumstances of conflict inside prison:

> *When people show anger and malice*
> *I vow with all beings*
> *to listen for truth in the message,*
> *ignoring the way it is said.* [15]

When we are the object of the negativity of others, we usually fail to see the fear or insecurity that sent that emotion in our direction. All behavior means something. What might the anger of this other person mean? Another Aitken gatha:

> *When anger or sadness arises*
> *I vow with all beings*
> *to accept my emotional nature—*
> *it's how I embody the Tao.* [16]

(*Tao* is a transliteration of the Chinese word for "Way." It is pronounced "dow.") When we make a commitment to an ethical way of life, we will find ourselves constantly disappointed in our own thoughts and behavior. A gatha like this one acknowledges that our own moods, irrational thoughts, and actions are the raw materials of our practice. This is *practice*—not perfection. Compassion, forgiveness, and acceptance must begin with ourselves. Forgiving our own constant failings allows us to forgive others.

Try inventing some gathas for the circumstances of your own daily life. For example,

> *When that guard I don't like comes on duty,*

> *I vow with all beings*
> *to honor his humanity*
> *and to befriend my own negative emotions.*

Stepping out of the power game is an act of great maturity. It means giving up our desire to control other people or conditions. It means giving up our righteous belief in our own rightness. It especially means recognizing greed, hatred, and ignorance in our own thoughts, words, and actions. Recognize and let go. Recognize and let go. This is how mindfulness works itself into the details of our daily lives.

CHAPTER 3 NOTES

1. Gunaratna Sarika, Ohio State Prison inmate, personal communication, 1997.
2. The *kyôsaku* is a wooden stick used as a "cautionary device" (the literal meaning of the term) in the meditation halls of some Zen lineages. It is used to "wake up" meditators who might be inclined to doze or indulge in distractions. They are hit once on the shoulder muscles on each side of the neck. The kyôsaku makes a big noise but does no physical harm if applied properly. In most U.S. Zen centers the stick is administered by the meditation hall monitor only when the recipient requests the blows. For a deeper explanation of this device, see Robert Aitken, *Taking the Path of Zen*, 37-39.
3. Kobutsu (Kevin) Malone, personal communication, 1997.
4. Kusala Ratnakaruna, personal communication, 1998.
5. John Daido Loori, "Lotus in the Fire: Prison, Practice, and Freedom," typescript, n.d., 2.
6. Malone.
7. Geoffrey Shugen Arnold, personal communication, 1997.
8. A *rakusu* is a biblike vestment worn around the neck in certain Japanese Zen lineages. It is given at the time of *jukai* (refuge ceremony) or at monastic ordinations. On its reverse side is a calligraphy of the initiate's new Buddhist name and the signature of the teacher leading the ceremony.
9. Arnold.
10. Ibid.
11. Henepola Gunaratana, *Mindfulness in Plain English* (Boston: Wisdom Publications, 1992), 166.
12. Fleet Maull, "Dharma in Hell," *Shambhala Sun*, March 1993, 26.
13. Greenwell, personal communication.
14. I don't know which translation of the *Dhammapada* Parker read. These excerpts are from Thomas Cleary, *Dhammapada: The Sayings of Buddha* (New York: Bantam Books 1994), 7-14.
15. Robert Aitken, *The Dragon Who Never Sleeps: Verses for Zen Buddhist Practice* (Berkeley: Parallax Press, 1992), 18.
16. Aitken, *Dragon*, 35.

Good Behavior:
Precepts for Insiders

A satori which is unrelated to your personal character is nothing more than a kind of drunkenness.[1]
                                                        —Kosho Uchiyama

Enlightenment *(satori* in Japanese) is the experience of release from the causes of suffering and from the delusion of an independent self. But it cannot be measured by any lab procedure or paper-pencil test. Its evidence is in the real world. So the goal of practice is not some kind of sedation but, rather, the harmonious, value-driven interplay between action and stillness—all while living in the suffering world.

With good reason, religious conversion inside prison is often looked upon with skepticism by prison authorities as well as by other inmates. Acting out a conversion is often seen as part of a campaign to acquire more letters of recommendation for the parole board and to impress those in power. Conversion may be a game of troubling insincerity. So the real test of any spirituality comes only with evidence of behavior in the real world. And real conversion is always in process, always imperfect, always trying to refine itself. It is never a done deal. San Quentin inmate Jarvis Masters writes "In prison, no one believes that conversion to religion is real. Most prisoners think that anyone who suddenly catches religion is playing a game or trying to con their way out of the system. Inmates distance themselves from religous prisoners, believing religion will make them weak." [2]

Chapter 2 ended with a recitation of the ten grave precepts, which are a mahayana elaboration of the traditional five lay precepts, common to all of Buddhism. These five precepts are just as important for our Buddhist identity as is the practice of sitting still.

Even though meditation is the core—the center of our Buddhist lives—our thoughts, speech, and behavior must also reflect the intentions contained in that quiet sitting. The precepts remind us of these intentions. These five principles of conduct—or vows, or trainings—are the bottom-line behavioral boundaries that all Buddhists are expected to adhere to. They were called *pañcha sîla* in Sanskrit, translated by Buddhist scholar Roger Corless as "the five rules of restraint." Here is his rendering:

> 1. I take upon myself the discipline of abstaining from harming sentient beings.
> 2. I take upon myself the discipline of abstaining from taking that which is not offered.
> 3. I take upon myself the discipline of abstaining from sexual misconduct.
> 4. I take upon myself the discipline of abstaining from false speech.
> 5. I take upon myself the discipline of abstaining from stupefying drink.[3]

Many westerners, including myself, were first attracted to the more distilled forms of Buddhism, like Zen, because these seemed free of the ornate and oppressive moral theologies of the three major forms of monotheism: Islam, Judaism, and Christianity. And, in fact, Buddhism has no god who issues commandments, or anything else; it is a religion without a supreme being and, therefore, a religion without a theology. In the iconoclastic 1960s and 1970s, many of us seemed to think that Buddhism was a grand intuitive method that encouraged the yoga of meditation but had nothing to say about the rest of our lives. We were relieved to find a religion that seemed to have no *thou shalt nots*.

What we did not understand is that the precepts are the method through which meditation practice becomes life. They are often thought of as preconditions for being "on the path." After doing meditation for a number of years you will begin to get the impression that the precepts come out of (are created by) the act of sitting still. This is because meditation creates an increasing sophistication about the workings of your own mind; this awareness continues with you throughout your day in the world. You begin to notice, for instance, how you subtly distort your own speech with other people—altering the truth slightly (or enormously) to make yourself look good and to make others look less impressive. You start to see your own cravings—for sex or food or attention or possessions—run out of control and propel you into distraction or, ultimately, into harmful actions. The changes in behavior that come from increasing mindfulness are subtle but pervasive.

In another sense, the precepts are a precondition of sitting still. You cannot make your living as a hit man, for instance, and sit down to zazen every day expecting to make some kind of spiritual progress. The gradual clarity that comes from repeatedly looking at mind would make such actions as murder intolerable to a person who is beginning to see the world with more accuracy. The desperate fondness we have for our "self" gradually begins to decrease. This means that we no longer have to churn up greed or aggression to feed or defend this hungry and frightened (but totally imagined) ego. Here is another exercise:

MEDITATION SEVEN: THE MOVING SELF
Sit, following the instructions for posture given in chapter 2. Continue the one-to-ten exhalation count but focus your attention on the tip of your nose, where the moving air of your inhalations and exhalations passes. Notice the exact feeling inside your nose and the sense of the air coming in, to be part of you, and then leaving, taking part of you outside. Move the center of your self-awareness from your brain to the tip of your nose. Now bring that awareness lower, to the diaphragm in your abdomen that controls this breathing.

Experience the ebb and flow of your breathing as it gets more gentle and regular. Think of the rise and fall of the breath as gentle ocean swells. Try this for ten minutes.

Meditation is not just a head trip—it is a yoga, a physical discipline of the whole body and mind. Where does your self end? Is it at the tip of your nose? Or is it at the end of a phone line when you are talking to relatives or friends? Is your mind the same as your brain? There are other possibilities. I once heard a Japanese Zen master speak, and each time he said the English word "mind," he used his left hand to tap his abdomen (*hara* in Japanese), which is indeed where Japanese culture envisions the center of personal awareness. An American or European speaker would have tapped his or her head at each use of the same word. Meditation gradually teaches us that our own culturally taught sense of self is very limited.

The garbageman who bangs the can against his truck each morning while I am meditating is also a part of my intimacy with the world, and my silent breathing is a part of his. When we meditate, are our tingling feet less important than our buzzing thoughts or the blaring radio from two cells down? Who can say? This is why the historical Buddha got up from under the bodhi tree with the realization that there is no abiding self and that all phenomena are related. That relationship is explained by the principle of "dependent co-arising," which means that no thing exists by itself. There is no peace, for instance, without the reality of conflict. There is no sun without earth and moon and Venus. There is no prison without the reality of freedom in the outside world. There is no desert without the forest. Land and ocean need each other. Nothing is truly independent of the rest of the world.

These realizations bring the Buddhist practitioner toward an ethical stance that seems similar to the "do unto others" golden rule of Christianity. I say *seems* because there is a difference. The golden rule is a simile: treat others *as if* they were you. The Buddhist version, however, is an equation: treat others well because they *are* you. The universe is self. The mind is universe, and, as the great Zen ancestor Bodhidharma taught,

"The mind's capacity is limitless, and its manifestations are inexhaustible. Seeing forms with your eyes, hearing sounds with your ears, smelling odors with your nose, tasting flavors with your tongue, every movement or state is your mind. At every moment, where language can't go, that's your mind." [4]

Our sitting still should be seen as a benefit not only to ourselves but also to others. With this understanding as our context, I would like to focus on the five core precepts of Buddhism from the point of view of practice in a prison environment. The precepts may be thought of as vows or resolutions that we take publicly in front of other Buddhists; this is exactly the format of the refuge ceremony. We make a commitment to train, using the precepts to coach ourselves. Taking the precepts publicly, however, is not just an individual act witnessed by others. The precepts are really the shared intentions of the whole sangha, the Buddhist community, and we help each other to stay true to these behavioral goals. Gunaratna Sarika caught on to this idea in his practice with another Buddhist inmate. "Sometimes we just call out a precept number to each other to remind ourselves what is the right thing to do in a given situation." [5]

FIRST PRECEPT: NOT KILLING

The Judeo-Christian commandment "Thou shalt not kill" was meant to refer to the taking of human life, whereas the Buddhist precept refers to all sentient beings, including cockroaches and mosquitoes. The Buddhist precept also makes no allowances for the killing of humans by the state—whether in war or by capital punishment.

Most prisoners who have killed—except for contract and serial killers—did so in a fit of anger, rage, or jealousy; and often the person they killed was someone close and even dear to them. To kill another human being often means killing that person in thought first. That's why propaganda is needed to help soldiers believe that the people they are killing are the "enemy"—not just ordinary human beings. Governments can kill prisoners because they are "felons" or "murderers," a change in identity that allows the state to hold public murders (renamed "executions") with few moral qualms.

So, too, a wife or girlfriend who we feared was cheating on us might have been killed because we switched to calling her something else: "slut," for example, instead of "honey." By making someone our enemy, we also make the mental adjustment needed to give ourselves permission to kill. The practice of insight and compassion that is at the heart of Buddhism requires us not only to give up the physical act of killing but also to work on its root cause: the thoughts that prepare the way for violence.

Everyone, inmate or free—except perhaps for the most saintly of us—has occasional violent fantasies. On the outside, these probably occur most frequently when we are driving our cars. Inside prisons, inmates often focus violent thoughts on cruel guards or on other inmates who are noisy, crazy, or violent—or on inmates of another race. Sometimes the desire to hurt or kill is focused on someone outside, a prosecutor or a cop, an ex-boyfriend or girlfriend, an abusive parent—anyone who we feel really hurt us and who we think deserves our retribution.

If these thoughts become too strong, they will intrude into your meditation. Intrusive thoughts, whether violent or just distracting, don't go away by just trying not to think them. (Try *not thinking* of a green elephant and see what image comes immediately to mind.) Sometimes it is best to address the dark side of mind directly in order to diffuse these powerful thoughts of killing or harm. The precept not to kill, therefore, is more than a prohibition not to commit a murder; it is also a training device to help us tame the violence in our thoughts. Strong violent thoughts might mean therapy is needed, perhaps in conjunction with a more psychological, insight-based form of meditation.

Here is a way to train oneself out of violent thoughts. It comes from the vipassana tradition and works in the same way as do gathas (the short poems mentioned in chapter 3, which are meant to remind us of our best intentions). Whenever you notice a negative thought regarding another person, have a gatha or *metta* (a technique to help us wish others well) formula ready to counteract your negativity. For instance, as you are standing in line you notice that you are thinking about what a jerk the prisoner standing in front of you is. As soon as you catch the thought, stop. Now say to yourself: "I want him to be safe; I want him to be healthy, and I want him to find happiness." This is the same thing you would wish for yourself, or your children, or anyone else you love. Try making up your own counteractive poems or sayings. "May this guard who is being unfair to me discover justice. May his fear turn into peace and his unhappiness into contentment." Remember once again that this is practice, not perfection. The negative or violent thoughts are often habitual and will not disappear overnight. The idea is to start noticing them as they appear and turning them around. This is the hard work of removing the mental roots of killing.

As I mentioned in chapter 1, the historical Buddha confronted the murderer Angulimala, who had terrorized the people of a certain town. The Buddha met him on the empty streets of an Indian village that had been abandoned by its frightened citizens, in a kind of *High Noon* encounter that stands out in its drama from more mundane sutra stories. In the showdown, the Buddha challenge Angulimala to change his life, adopt a heart of compassion, and begin to protect the lives of all living beings. But the murderer came up with a standard "con" excuse that shows us how far back in time this form of prison thinking goes:

> "Human beings do not love each other. Why should I love other people? Humans are cruel and deceptive. I will not rest until I have killed them all."
>
> The Buddha spoke gently, "Angulimala, I know you have suffered deeply at the hands of other humans. Sometimes humans can be most cruel. Such cruelty is the result of ignorance, hatred, desire, and jealousy. . . . Hatred is the path you are on now. You should stop. Choose the path of forgiveness, understanding, and love instead."
>
> The monk looked at Angulimala as if he considered him a whole person worthy of respect. Could this monk be the very Gautama he had heard people praise, the one they called "the Buddha?" Angulimala asked, "Are you

85

the monk Gautama?" The Buddha nodded.

Angulimala said, "It is a great pity I did not meet you sooner. I have gone too far already on my path of destruction. It is no longer possible to turn back." [6]

This is such a typical con dialogue that I smile whenever I read it. First Angulimala gives an excuse for his crimes, which amounts to "other people are bad, too, and they've been cruel to me." Then, when confronted with the possibility of change, he gives an excuse for not changing, subtly suggesting that it's the Buddha's fault for not meeting him sooner. But the monk Gautama doesn't give up on his insistence that Angulimala begin anew. At the end of this story, Angulimala takes refuge and is ordained as a monk. This is a skillful intervention on the part of the Buddha and makes good reading for anyone involved in prison dharma work. The Buddha is direct but accepting; he is sympathetic but challenging. He can also be fearless, simply because, unlike most of us, he has learned not to cling greedily to his own life.

The Buddha's message is simple: Angulimala's previous acts of murder do not prevent him from the possibility of waking up to the world, to the Four Noble Truths, and to the Eightfold Path. The monk Gautama knew that the intimacy with world and self that is generated by practice, by sitting still, could eventually lead Angulimala to protect all life.

NOT KILLING AND THE MIDDLE WAY

Yet to live is to kill. Corn and wheat plants die for our breakfast; birds are displaced and endangered by the roads and buildings set up to accommodate our human lives. Pigs squeal horribly as they are sacrificed to become cans of Spam for human consumption. Cows form sullen lines as machines with hoses pull out the milk that was meant to feed their calves.

To continue to live is to compromise with the injunction not to kill. Trying to avoid this compromise, Jains, a sect in India, sweep the roads before them so as not to step on any creatures, and they wear masks over their noses and mouths to keep from breathing in and inadvertently killing flying insects. But the historical Buddha taught a middle way, distant both from the obsessive ascetic path of nonkilling and from the carelessness of the warrior carnivore at the other extreme.

Not to kill, in terms of diet, might mean becoming a vegetarian. Buddhist monks and many earnest Buddhist laypeople avoid eating meat. Yet this practice has never been an absolute. Tibetan Buddhists, for instance, have always eaten meat products because fruits and vegetables were not available at the high altitudes where they lived. Monks are often told to eat whatever is given to them, even if fish or meat is put into their begging bowls.

On his way by car to Tassajara monastery one summer, Suzuki Roshi heard some Zen students in the back seat (apparently feeling proud of their own new-found vegetarianism) talking about what terrible people meat-eaters are. When the group stopped for lunch at a cafe along the California coastal highway, Suzuki Roshi ordered a steak. What was he teaching?

Becoming a vegetarian in a prison setting can turn into a bureaucratic nightmare and often requires many special permissions and much documentation. But becoming a vegetarian can be worth the effort. Some Buddhist prisoners eat whatever is given; others just refuse the main meat dishes. If fruit, vegetables, and grain are sufficient in the prison diet, this change may be accomplished with little effort and no damage to health. Avoiding all meat products in such things as soup bases, sauces, and baked goods becomes very much more complicated. But prison administrations may be slowly changing in regard to dietary offerings. The food service departments of institutions in some states, like Ohio, now have vegetarian alternatives—both vegan (no animal products at all) and ovo-lacto (including dairy products and eggs)—at every meal. Remember that all dietary practices are compromises. To stop all killing is to stop all eating.

Eating mindfully and gratefully may be as important a practice as refraining from eating any particular food. Writing in the Vermont Zen

Center's publication, *Walking Mountains*, Washington state inmate Calvin Malone talks about a practice he invented, which we can all try:

> I went to lunch in the dining hall. When I got my tray of food, I was greatly surprised to see the most beautiful green apple on my tray. This apple made me feel happy! It was large, with a stem. The skin was tight and the shape was perfect. It held the promise of delicious crispness. As I walked the quarter mile back to my room, I held the apple in the flat of my left palm, and did Apple Meditation. . . . Once inside my room, I began to think about the apple's long journey just to get to me. The seed, the growing and care of the tree. I thought about the minerals in the ground, the sun and water and all the things that helped make this beautiful apple. I became very mindful of this apple. I saw all the people involved in growing and transporting my apple. . . . Finally I was faced with a decision—to eat or not to eat the apple. . . . I ate it. It was delicious! [7]

Malone discovered one of the important points in the Buddhist attitude toward not killing and consumption, which is that we need to be gratefully aware of how food comes to us. In Japanese Buddhist traditions, during intensive retreats, we often eat *oryoki-* style, which requires special interlocking bowls and ritual movements throughout the meal. This is a fascinating and beautiful practice, but not easy. Oryoki trains us to slow down, to be reverent to our food and to our utensils, and to be aware of those around us who are also eating.

Mindful eating can be accomplished in prison, if only by a slight bow to the food on our metal tray. This gesture reminds us of the human, animal, and plant effort that has brought the food to us. If there is meat on your tray and you want to eat it, you can at least say a brief grace or poem before eating.

Here is a poem written by Zen Master Zenshin Philip Whalen called *Grace Before Meat:*

> *You food, you animal plants*
> *I take you, now, I make you wise*
> *Beautiful and great with joy*
> *Enlightenment for all sentient beings*
> *All the hungry spirits, gods and buddhas who are sad* [8]

SECOND PRECEPT: NOT TAKING WHAT IS NOT OFFERED

The original precept not only prohibited active stealing, but it also said we should not take anything not offered. In other words, it also prohibited the act of asking someone for something of theirs that we might or might not need ourselves. Worded in this way, the precept would also prohibit keeping something we have found—a dollar bill on the ground, for instance—as it was never offered to us.

The underground economies that operate inside prisons are filled with any number of transactions including thefts, borrowings, gifts with no strings, barters, swaps, and cash sales. The goods that change hands in these transactions may be anything from a stick of gum to a human life.

How do the results of sitting change our dealings in this underground economic world? This precept or intention has refraining from active theft as its bottom line only; its true import is as training toward generosity. Just as the first precept, not to kill, has refraining from murders as its bottom line but intends much more than that, so the second precept also intends more. Generosity may be achieved not only with money or the distribution of goods but can also be practiced with such things as our time and our talents. To help another inmate write a letter or sew a button on a shirt is just as much an enactment of this vow as the act of refraining from stealing that same inmate's shirt.

Robbery, theft, embezzlement, shoplifting, credit card fraud, and other crimes related to greed and property are often what land us in prison in the first place. Sometimes this greed is related to addiction or poverty, sometimes not. But whatever the dynamics of the original offense, the inmate who wants to become a Buddhist practitioner must learn to deal honestly and without greed in the prison environment. We need to start surrounding our transactions involving others with honesty and with generous intentions. This is not easy to do.

THIRD PRECEPT: NOT MISUSING SEX

This precept or intention is very related to the previous two. Unchecked sexual activity can be a form of greed in which the objects of desire are numberless. It can also be a form of killing when we violate the integrity of others by forcing sex on them against their will. That force may be in the form of overt violence, or we might—more subtly—use age, rank, or wealth to get what we want. Sexual misconduct can also be a form of killing where relationships are involved, especially when it takes the form of adultery. In general, I would not call Buddhism antisexual, as are some of the monotheisms. Nor would I call Buddhism sex-affirmative. Except for this general lay precept, and some detailed rules for monks and nuns, Buddhist writings are generally silent on sexual issues.

Inmates who are in prison for sexual offenses have an obligation to examine honestly what happened and to do everything possible to alter this behavior. Such work can be accomplished through therapy, self-help reading, or participation in twelve-step programs. Sometimes medications that lower libido (sexual drive) might also be considered if there seems to be a biological base for the offenses.

Sex inside prison is another matter. This issue forms part of the public stereotype of the prison environment, and custodial staffs and police seem oddly obsessed about it. But a well-run prison has a minimum of same-sex rapes. When rape does happen, good institutions make sure there are consequences for the aggressor and protection for the victim.

Poorly run institutions collude in the culture of power and violence that encourages this form of loveless aggression. Sometimes sex can be bought or sold by inmates for money or other favors. Sometimes sex between inmates is voluntary and even, occasionally, based on real love and respect for each other. But sex in U.S. prisons is often clouded by the dread of being labeled homosexual—which is anathema to the way most men are socialized in U.S. culture. Power differences serve to compensate for this dread, as in the status distinction in prison culture between "shooters" and "catchers"—as if being the "active" participant in sex were a badge of manhood.

One book about how to survive in prison gives instructions on how to fashion and conceal a knife so as to defend against prison rape. I don't recommend the book or the practice. A pamphlet that was in circulation in U.S. prisons in 2001 recommended that new inmates make informed choices about sexual protection and "negotiate" with prospective "jockeys," or "old men," as they are called in some prisons. The new "catcher" would thus be assured protection from other contenders for his allegiance and would, in essence, settle for the "best deal" in terms of the expectations of the relationship. Some such arrangements involve virtual servitude to the dominant partner; others are more mutual. I find it hard to wholeheartedly recommend this second strategy, even though it is a more skillful and potentially less violent solution to the newcomer's problem.

Exploitation of another prisoner by force is clearly prohibited by the third precept. Taking advantage of another prisoner's youth, physical weakness, ignorance or poverty to gratify sexual greed is also against this precept. Sex provided for money or goods, while seemingly voluntary, is rarely so. In other words, the rationale of payment does not make sexual transactions just, because the poverty of the one is forced to submit to the relative wealth or power of the other.

Prison sexual assault prevention programs can be started by inmates themselves, even if administrations seem unresponsive to the need. Older, more experienced prisoners can watch over and help prevent the physical and sexual abuse of other prisoners—especially of the newest or the weakest. Jarvis Masters, in his book, *Finding Freedom*, gives a moving account of how his growing awareness of Buddhist ethics helped him prevent the assault of a homosexual prisoner—at some risk to his own reputation and safety.

When a young, inexperienced prisoner enters an institution, he often has no money to purchase needed toiletries, cigarettes, or other supplies. If the prison has a work program, he has not had time to build any money on a canteen account and spouses or family often are out of contact or too poor to contribute. This poverty of almost all new inmates makes them vulnerable to sexual exploitation with the gift or promise of goods in exchange for sex. Thus, experienced prisoners with connections can sometimes commit themselves to preventing such exploitation by gathering supplies for newcomers which, when provided without strings, can help prevent one of the prime motivations for the trade in sexual favors. Such actions by prison sangha members would also be a way of putting this third precept into positive action, rather than just considering it a "thou shalt not."

Controversy over pornography is another ongoing prison issue that relates to the third precept. Some freedom of speech advocates have won prison cases against administrations that censored inmate subscriptions to magazines like *Playboy* or *Hustler*. Some criminal justice administrators say that visual pornography incites lust, while others hold that such publications probably lessen the chances of sexual acting out, as they are used primarily for the purpose of masturbation. They are even called "stroke mags" in prison jargon. Those concerned with the exploitation of women contend that all such visual images in pornographic publications are degrading and exploitative. There are good arguments on both sides of this controversy.

Masturbation is the most common prison sexual behavior. And, as long as the Buddhist practitioner has not taken more extensive monastic vows, the wording of the third precept does not seem to prohibit this behavior. No relationship is broken or harmed, and—as long as no addictive pattern is formed (which would include a pattern of obsessive thoughts, craving, release, dissatisfaction, then resumption of obsession)— masturbation may represent a valid expression of the middle way of Buddhist behavior. Self-pleasure could also be looked at as sexual behavior taking place in the context of a loving relationship with self—if indeed the practitioner has gained some basic sense of self-esteem. Some Buddhist teachers do suggest that sexual energy is best conserved and redirected into meditation practice, yet there is no universal Buddhist teaching on masturbation. For those in prison, it seems one of the least complicated, and least harmful, outlets for sexual energy.

In some Buddhist traditions, monks are trained to meditate on images of dead human bodies or of human fluids and viscera. These are not merely exercises in revulsion but are meant, rather, as reminders of impermanence. Despite what the love songs say, human love is not forever, nor is attraction, nor is physical beauty. How we handle our sexuality as Buddhists is one of the best indications of character maturity. Can we live as sexual beings without the fanaticisms of puritanical aversion and without the reckless pursuit of sexual pleasure that harms or exploits others? The introspection involved in meditation practice can help us to be honest about sexual feelings and motives as we discover them in our mental experience. Most of us habitually distort these feelings by calling them love or (especially in the prison setting) by seeing them as the self-enhancing exercise of power over others. The disciplines of meditation and mindfulness also help us to experience the fact that we can have sexual thoughts without being compelled to act on them. Sex can be greed; it can be aggression; it can be consensual pleasure; it can even be a way of expressing genuine love. Our practice will help us to distinguish honestly which of these we are experiencing.

Some conservative Buddhists, like some conservative Christians, condemn homosexuality and masturbation. Early Buddhist writings do contain prohibitions about sex at the wrong time, the wrong place, or in the wrong orifice. To this day, the Dalai Lama has cited these writings in his dialogues with gay Buddhist practitioners and has declined to endorse homosexual behavior as permissible. Other Buddhist teachers have come to other conclusions. To figure this out for ourselves, we must continue to invoke the concept of the middle way. Buddhist teachings are never immune to the biases of the cultures from which they arise— the cultural biases, for instance, of a Tibetan monastic class or of an educated, secular humanist American middle class. The middle way suggests that we not be overly puritanical nor overly permissive.

FOURTH PRECEPT: NOT SPEAKING FALSELY

Buddhism has always been concerned with the ethics of speech. Aitken Roshi told me once that the Hindu ideal of "gentle speech" was already a part of the cultural and ethical environment in which the historical Buddha taught. Right speech is one of the eight elements of the Eight-fold Path.

In Buddhist thinking, speech is on an equal plane with thought and conduct, because speech can kill or it can encourage. Words can wound or revive. Words have consequences. We also speak silently, day in and day out, through the thoughts in our minds. This is one of the first things the beginning meditator notices: how much time during meditation is spent listening to our own internal speech. Our monkey minds chatter away about this and that. Meditation is a great opportunity to work on this precept—by monitoring and observing our internal speech and learning to change negative thoughts before they come out of our mouths as harsh words. We eventually also learn to quiet the chatter of thoughts.

The bottom line of this precept is not lying, yet much more is involved in right speech as a Buddhist training. This precept also warns us against gossip, one of the most pervasive activities in any prison or in any human group. Gossip may be defined as the "spread of news that I do not know to be certain." And gossip can be dangerous in prisons. Malicious speech can ruin someone's reputation faster than any other sort of behavior. Distorted stories passed on unquestioningly may incite violence against fellow inmates or against guards. Some inmates become masters of gossip and use it to get their way or to cause division and discord among those they see as their enemies.

Stereotyped name calling—usually with racial, or sexual, themes—is also common in prisons and violates the spirit of the fourth precept. These epithets are always putdowns, words that can kill the energy and self-respect of others. Custodial staff sometimes are guilty of this kind of destructive speech, calling names or mocking certain inmates or participating enthusiastically in the spread of gossip.

Destructive speech often becomes habitual, and, when this is the case, the practice of the fourth precept is even more of a challenge. But words exist in our thoughts first, before they are vocalized, so meditation is a good opportunity to watch the words that habitually come to mind.

In the extension of the five lay precepts into the ten grave precepts, four of the five additional mahayana precepts have some relationship to speech: don't speak ill of others; don't promote oneself while disparaging others; don't dwell in anger; and don't defame the Buddha, dharma or sangha. These additional precepts add subtleties to the Buddhist ethics of speech. Namedropping ("as I was saying when I visited the Dalai Lama") and bragging ("I have a Ph.D. and I drive a BMW") are against these precepts. Dwelling on the faults of others, even if everything you say about them is absolutely true, is also against these teachings.

In the full realization of "no-self," we begin to understand that talking about the faults of others is actually talking about ourselves. Negative speech creates a permanent trace or image of that person in your mind, as well as in the mind of the person you are speaking to. Negative talk about another also freezes that person into a negative identity—as if he or she will never change, as if there is no hope for anyone to become anything but the way we perceive him or her right now.

The practice of right speech is a full-time endeavor that includes our time in meditation as well as our time going about our daily lives. This practice can be especially powerful when it begins to spread within an institution, whether that place is a prison or a corporate office. When I speak to prison dharma groups, I almost always focus on right speech. Right speech enables peacemaking, lessens tensions, encourages people. And the flip side of speaking, which is listening, must not be forgotten either. How often do we treat what someone is saying as an interruption to our own speech. The practice of active listening—paying close attention to what someone is saying—is also a practice of right speech. Right speech is a rich field for practice.

FIFTH PRECEPT: NOT TO USE OR DEAL IN INTOXICANTS

Paul Dewey, a practitioner of Tibetan Buddhism and inmate at Folsom prison in California, writes in a letter about his practice and its relation to his history of substance abuse. "The biggest barriers and difficulties that I face practicing inside are of my own making. I've blamed other people, conditions, time constraints, etc., for problems that I've had maintaining focus in study, meditation, and visualization. The truth of the matter is that it is me: plain and simple. When I was getting loaded many years ago, there was nothing that could stop me: I got stoned come hell or high water." [9]

One of the things to notice in Dewey's comment is that he is honest about his own responsibility for his practice and for maintaining the sobriety that must support that practice. There is no one else to blame for being in prison, for not practicing, or for drinking and drugging. This is the voice of a mature practice that accepts and works on this precept.

In Buddhist meditation, we must continually accept our distractions and return to our visualizations or our breath counting, just as we must accept the desire to scratch our nose or wiggle our toes while sitting. In the same way, we must accept our histories, our faults, and our skills. We accept the fact that we just lost count and must return to "one." This process, practiced while sitting, can eventually move us to accept bigger things, like our own role in being in prison or in a history of substance abuse or in our mistreatment of others.

Suzuki Roshi once told someone that alcoholism is a very strict practice. This is true of all addictions. Addiction has been seen by some theorists as an attempt to experience peace as well as pleasure, to make the world feel right internally. In part, this is the same purpose that brings many of us to dharma practice. Addiction is a practice in the sense that, like meditation, it is done over and over again—and you never quite get it right.

The people who are at risk for addiction are those whose drinking or drugging makes them feel normal or at home in the world. It is as if the use of alcohol or drugs restores some internal balance. But, of course, drugs and alcohol create serious and damaging neurological changes that distort thinking and unleash the primary emotions (rage, jealousy, fear, lust) in ways that the neocortex of the brain can no longer control. This is the process called "limbic kindling," which is the physiology behind many, if not most, crimes of violence that result in incarceration. Statistics vary, but it is safe to say that more than 50 percent of those in prison were intoxicated at the time they committed their crimes. Paul Dewey writes:

> I was chairman of our A.A. group at Mule Creek Prison [California] for five years. One night I was walking the yard with another member who was paroling soon. He was scared and really unsure if he could stay sober and keep from picking up a violation. So I gave him the best advice that I knew, and as I was telling him I heard myself speaking almost as if someone else were speaking to me.
>
> You have to decide what you want most. You can't get loaded and stay out of here. One leads to the other, so you have to want one more than the other. So what do you want most? To get stoned? Or to stay out of prison? Whichever one that you want most is what you'll base your attitude and your actions on and those will be the results that you get. Right then I knew I'd hit the nail on the head. [10]

For inmates with a history of addiction, participation in prison Alcoholics Anonymous or Narcotics Anonymous meetings is in the spirit of this precept. Step eleven of the twelve steps is that we "sought through prayer and meditation to improve our conscious contact with God as we understood him." Meditation and twelve-step recovery go hand-in-hand. Inmates with substance-abuse histories have an ethical duty to themselves and to others to learn as much about their addictions as possible and to maintain sobriety, both inside prison and when they get out.

Drugs and/or alcohol are available in most prison underground economies, so the commitment to recovery can begin inside. This commitment does not have to wait to be tested on release.

Like meditation practice, the twelve-step recovery programs focus on undistorting the ego and on the development of honesty with self and others. Meditation, the precepts, and the twelve recovery steps can work together. No one can make progress in meditation if he or she is actively practicing his or her addiction. (Anyone who has ever tried to do sitting meditation with a hangover could testify to how unpleasant the experience can be.) Most people in the recovering community also feel that it is very hard to recover from an addiction without a commitment to spiritual progress.

An issue that often comes up in prisons about this precept concerns the use of psychiatric medications. Every prison has its share of mentally ill inmates. Indeed, the U.S. prison system is the largest (and most dysfunctional) mental health system in the country. Many inmates need psychiatric medications for a variety of conditions, the most common of which are schizophrenia, bipolar disorder, attention deficit disorder, and depression. Studies also show that many inmates, particularly in the most secure facilities, have various forms of brain damage, mostly as a result of head trauma of various sorts.

Medications may be distinguished from drugs of abuse because they are given in consultation with experts and are meant to heal rather than entertain or provide escape. But many inmates who legitimately need such medicines refuse them or avoid taking them because they are embarrassed that others will know about their condition. Such inmates are often put down and teased mercilessly by their fellows; they may eventually give up trying to get appropriate care and instead retreat into a form of macho denial by telling themselves they should be able to handle things on their own. Buddhist sanghas within institutions could think of ways to help members or other prisoners who suffer from these medical conditions.

Prison sanghas also need to provide help for each other to examine the full implications of this precept in terms of such substances as candy, cigarettes, coffee—and even to examine the all-too-common American addiction to staring at the electromagnetic flickering of television sets. Addiction is a strict practice: we train ourselves to engage in it automatically, day after day, with a steady loss of contact with the real present moment and with the real needs of the world around us. Yet, with support, we can train ourselves out of addiction by using Buddhist practices along with professional treatment and twelve step participation.

PRECEPT PRACTICE

In some lineages of Chinese Buddhism, laypeople may take the precepts in a refuge ceremony and leave out one or more of the five or ten precepts—depending on the version they are using. The idea is that it is better not to take a precept at all than to make a vow and then not keep it. A man who wanted to keep going to brothels would just skip the third precept. A woman who wanted to continue making her living as a tavern keeper would take refuge but skip the fifth precept. Perhaps there is sound logic behind their thinking.

The fruits of Buddhist practice must be seen in the real world, not in some exotic mental event that produces a so-called enlightenment. Long years of meditation are no guarantee of good behavior. The precepts must be co-equal with—or even a precondition of—meditation practice. Each supports the other. If Buddhist practice in a prison setting is the job of a warrior, then the precepts are the warrior's rules of engagement. They are lines in the sand for our thoughts and behaviors. They are signposts leading us toward our own best but never perfect selves.

CHAPTER 4 NOTES

1. Kosho Uchiyama, *From the Zen Kitchen to Enlightenment* (New York: Weatherhill, 1994), 34.

2. Jarvis Jay Masters, *Finding Freedom: Writings from Death Row* (Junction City, Calif: Padma Publishing, 1997).

3. Roger Corless, *The Vision of Buddhism* (New York: Paragon House, 1989), 77.

4. Bodhidharma, *The Zen Teachings of Bodhidharma*, trans. Red Pine (San Francisco: North Point Press, 1987), 23.

5. Gunaratna Sarika, personal communication, 1997.

6. Thich Nhat Hanh, *Old Path White Clouds: Walking in the Footsteps of the Buddha* (Berkeley: Parallax Press, 1991), 353-55.

7. Calvin Malone, "Apple Meditation," *Walking Mountain* (Shelburne, Vt., February 1997).

8. Philip Whalen, *Canoeing up Cabarga Creek: Buddhist Poems* (Berkeley: Parallax Press, 1996), 39.

9. Paul Dewey, personal communication, 1997.

10. Ibid.

Enemy Yoga:
The Practice of Making Peace

Kindness and compassion are extremely important in every area of life, whether we are prisoners, prison guards or victims of crime. It is futile to harbor hatred and ill-will even toward those who abuse us. Cooperation, trust and consideration are far more constructive. The hostility and negativity of prison life will not change until both staff and inmates can improve their attitudes towards each other in this way.[1]

—The Dalai Lama

As inmates, we may think that we have enemies everywhere: outside prosecutors, inside guards, other inmates, members of the public who wait outside death-row walls and cheer when an inmate is executed. Prisoners are certainly the objects of the hatred of others—victims of crime, families of victims, and the police officers or prison guards who see it as their duty to punish. The public is also encouraged to fear crime and criminals, and it does—even as the yearly crime statistics go down, the fear and the hatred seem to increase against all logic.

One reason for this is that politicians often try to win votes by outdoing each other in how tough they are on crime and criminals. County sheriffs and city police chiefs sometimes see benefits to their budgets as a result of emphasizing the prevalence of crime. It's an easy way to drum up more money for everything from new flack jackets to higher officer pay.

101

Even though it cannot be said that prisoners are surrounded by love and compassion, it is nevertheless crucial that inmates wanting to practice Buddhism learn the skills of compassion. When we ourselves are the object of so much condemnation and hatred, when prisoners are so often seen as the Enemy, then we ourselves must work in the opposite direction.

What His Holiness the Dalai Lama once called "enemy yoga" is the effort to yoke (connect) body and mind in the practice of loving self and extending that love to every other person, being, and thing in the world. This practice starts with the effort to dispel even the idea of *enemy,* whether inside or outside ourselves. In the Buddhist map of the world, there is no individual release from suffering, no release for me alone or for you only. To re-form, we need to experience love of self and love of others—and we need to accomplish this in the seemingly loveless environment of a prison.

No Enemy

Enemy yoga begins in the effort both to reduce the number of enemies we think we have and to stop being enemies to ourselves and our neighbors. By constantly acting on our fears and hatreds, instead of on generosity and compassion, we keep churning the karma of hate.

There is a reason you or I are in prison. My personal estimate is that one in thirty inmates is actually innocent of the charges that resulted in incarceration. Yet even in these cases, there is a history to be examined—and always a benefit to our practice from that examination. Buddhism would characterize the actions that brought us to prison in one of the three classical categories (*poisons*): greed, hatred, ignorance. *Greed* means clinging to people or things; *hatred* means judging people or things negatively and pushing them away. These first two categories are fairly easy to understand, because we have all been aware of experiencing them.

The third condition, *ignorance,* is harder to deal with, because no one wants to admit to it. Ignorance, in the Buddhist sense of the term, has nothing to do with being smart or stupid. Although ignorance may be many things, it is especially the inability to stop the pushing and pulling, the clinging and aversion of greed and hatred that pervade our human lives. Ignorance is not just not knowing; it is also the failure to preserve or cultivate a clear mind. Ignorance is thinking I know my own mind, I don't need to change—I'll change tomorrow. Ignorance means believing our own stories about ourselves and believing the reasons we make up for our successes and the excuses for our failures.

Sitting still works on all three of these negative conditions of human life. It gives us practice in letting go of ideas and impulses. It allows the mind to clear and the "self to point a light at the self," as someone—I don't remember who—once said. Sitting still can also help us undistort the ego, by showing us that we are not all bad—and that we are not all innocent either. This undistortion of self allows knowledge to flourish. Thorough knowledge is the precursor for thorough love.

Americans are taught by the popular media, and especially by song lyrics, that love is mysterious and illogical. But love is not that mysterious. In his book *Teachings on Love*, Thich Nhat Hanh points out that love is made up of two main elements: knowledge and intention. To know yourself is to accept your past as well as your present. To know yourself thoroughly, without distortion, is to create the conditions in which real love may begin to flourish. This combination of knowing the world and knowing self and of intending compassion allows love to envelop our experience of the world. To know yourself in the full Buddhist sense is also to see that there is no self and no other. And if there is no other, there can be no enemy.

That vicious guard is you. That sneaky prosecutor or cheating girlfriend or sloppy cellmate is you. You must know them intimately—and that knowing will transform your hating into care. With more practice, that cautious care can become honest, openhearted love. This is a difficult alchemy, but it can be accomplished and it can help reform not just an individual life but a whole prison, a whole country, a whole universe.

Once you thoroughly know yourself, or another, you can begin to have the intention of well-being. This is the second element of love: that you want yourself and the other to be safe; to be happy and healthy; and to be free from suffering. We know from research that people do not naturally know how to love or how to empathize with another. Love and empathy must be modeled and taught by the adults in a child's life. Many people who commit crimes do so because they are unable to experience empathy—that is, identify with the feelings and needs of others. Some of us never had the opportunity to learn this quality. A Buddhist practice to help us with this problem is called *metta,* translated from the Pali language as "love" or "friendship."

Buddhism is full of numbered lists: the Four Noble Truths, the Eightfold Path, the three marks, the ten directions. Here is another short list of four called the *brahmaviharas,* meaning the "heavenly abodes" or "celestial homes." These are "limitless kindness" *(maitri),* compassion *(karuna),* joy *(mudita),* and equanimity *(upekkha).*

In my first interview with my first Zen teacher, he asked what I wanted. I remember saying that I wanted a home. This is not an unusual response, as most people looking for a spiritual path are hoping to feel at home in the world and in the life they have been given to live. Sitting still, and cultivating compassion, will lead to a home—an abode whose four walls may be thought of as the four brahmaviharas. This home is where you are headed, and finding yourself there is also how you will know when you have arrived. Can you rejoice in the good fortune and happiness of others? If so, this is mudita. Can you treat a good-looking, pleasant person and someone who is ugly and irritating and bigoted in the same way? If so, you are practicing upekkha. Practicing these are signs that will tell you that you are settling in your new abode.

ABODE ONE: LOVE

Most of us think we know what love means. But sometimes we mistake the insecurity of possessiveness for love, or sometimes we mistake a mixture of lust and longing for love. Usually we are just in the realm of obsession or infatuation. But for love to be real, it must be reality-based; that is why knowledge, or understanding, is such a big part of love. If we know someone— anyone—deeply enough, thoroughly enough, we would have no other choice but to love that person. Yes, even Hitler. Yes, even Jeffrey Dahmer. The Dalai Lama once said that we have to understand the suffering of the Germans during World War II. This was not a popular statement with many Israelis. Yet it was an important thing to say. Not politically correct, perhaps, but His Holiness was speaking from the standpoint of the very sound Buddhist principles embodied in the brahmaviharas. Maitri or metta, may seem appropriate when directed toward people who please us or toward people deserving of our sympathy, like the victims of the Holocaust and their families, but the real test of enemy yoga is to see if we can find understanding and positive intention (love) for those whose actions are evil or ignorant. No one of us can guarantee, for example, how we would have acted if put in the same situation as German citizens during World War II.

"I do not hate the Chinese," the Dalai Lama has said in public over and over again—despite the Chinese demographic genocide of the Tibetan people and the Chinese destruction of Buddhist monasteries and torture of monks, nuns, and laypeople.

This is enemy yoga: the skillful redirection of ignorance or evil or violence aimed at ourselves by others. This is the judolike skill of letting the aggressor lunge through you and on to the floor behind you. In a prison context, this yoga may be practiced by trying to understand the full context of the lives of members of other gangs or cliques, or the lives of custodial staff. After increasing understanding, we exercise the rest of metta by intending the other person well. We honestly want this person to be safe, happy, and healthy.

The four abodes are a practice—as well as a result of practice. A first attempt at understanding love might be by learning to receive it. Try this:

MEDITATION EIGHT: ACCEPTING LOVE

Sit in your zazen posture and count your breaths for a few minutes. As your breathing settles, think about anyone in your life who has ever loved you. (If

you are sure there has never been anyone in this category, imagine someone.)
Think about this person thinking of you. What does she appreciate? Why can
he love you, even though you have behaved badly at times? Don't interfere.
Let her love you. Let him forgive you. Let her appreciate and encourage you.
Notice how much your own feeling of well-being is increased by receiving this
love. Notice the warmth of the connection, the optimism and security that
you can feel from the force of someone else's love for you. Let it happen with-
out mental objections. Just receive; don't bargain. Just receive; don't judge or
argue. Just connect with this person who loves you. And be still.

ABODE TWO: COMPASSION

The Latin roots of the word "compassion" mean "feeling suffering together" with others. Compassion doesn't mean feeling sorry for; it doesn't
mean pity. If you see someone else hurt, can you feel his or her pain? If
so, you are moving toward your home—toward a life of "feeling with"
others.

The Pali word for compassion, *karuna*, has somewhat the sense of
the twin Christian concepts of charity and agape—communal rejoicing
mixed with a deep concern and love for others. In Buddhism, "others"
includes the nonhuman elements of the phenomenal world: ants and
warblers and rocks and weeds. Buddhism asks us to love more than just
the cuddly animals—like pandas and dolphins—it also commits us to
love rusty nails, broken glass, cockroaches, and metal food trays. There is
no picking and choosing in a world enlivened by compassion.

Think of the father who can't wait to attend the execution of his
daughter's killer. Think of him waiting in the observation area to watch
an inmate be killed through a one-way glass. Let yourself begin to understand his desire for vengeance, his grief, his lost hopes for his daughter's
future, his loneliness now. Can you see how to feel with this man? Can
you complete the process of loving him by intending that he be safe and
happy, by honestly wishing that he be released from his suffering?

Try another meditation:

MEDITATION NINE: WHO IS IT YOU HATE?

Sit in your meditation posture and count your exhalations for a few minutes. Let your breathing become smooth and deep. Now think of someone whom you have decided you hate. Notice in what ways that hating means pushing him away. What names do you call this person; what negative qualities do you assign to her? You probably have a list of her faults memorized. Review the list. Could any of your own thoughts or actions be described in the same words? Are there areas of that person's life you have never thought about? Have you seen him as he was when he was a child, a teenager, an infant? Do you think she ever suffered? Does anyone love him? Why would someone love him? What if YOU loved that person? What would happen? Is there a danger to you in doing this? If loving means knowing, then what do you still need to know about her or him?

Imagine sitting in the same quiet room alone with this person. Spend as much time in this room with him as you can. Don't say anything—don't accept or reject this person; just allow her to be in the same room with you. Pay attention to your own breathing. See if you can hear this person's breathing. Be still.

ABODE THREE: JOY

Does it sound funny to talk about joy in the prison setting? It does; yet it is possible. I experienced moments of great joy and tranquility while in prison. There were other moments and hours and days, of course, with other emotions. The abode of joy, though, is not talking about the ups and downs of our emotions.

Mudita, or joy, means the ability to experience the perfect quality of each moment. Through sitting still, we learn to accept our mind and our body, and this gradual practice of acceptance leads to joy. This is why one Zen master said, "Every day is a good day." This is not some happy-face slogan denying the difficulties of life. What he meant was that, clouds or sun, good mood or bad, every moment of every day can be accepted just as it is. And there is great joy in the ability to do this.

Discovering mudita also means being able to rejoice in the good fortune of others. This is an important measure of character refinement and cannot be easily accomplished without the awareness that comes from sitting still. Mudita may be the most difficult of the four abodes. Western philosophy and pop psychology teach us to value highly our personal autonomy and independence. We are encouraged to draw boundaries between our self and others. But this belief system in the western world is a far cry from the sense of interdependence and no abiding self that the historical Buddha discovered under the bodhi tree. It is with good reason that many traditional cultures in today's world accuse Euro-Americans of appearing to be selfish and overly aggressive in asserting personal boundaries and individual rights. It may be that we have gone down the wrong track in focusing on "self-esteem" and that Buddhist practice can remind us that there is an "other-esteem" also—that generosity is a more sure way to good self-feeling than the aggressive guarding of personal property, time, talents, and energy.

What if all our major real-world decisions were made, as some Native American traditions suggest, for the good of all of us, for the well-being of seven generations from now? What if we took the birds and fish and earthworms into consideration before we built any human structure? This is the broader meaning of mindfulness. This is the fullest practice of mudita. Walt Whitman said, "I contain multitudes"; as one of our finest American mystical poets, he was speaking for all of us. We all contain—are connected to—all others. There is no going it alone, even if you are a hermit.

The mahayana movement in Buddhism started in India in the first century A.D. It was a great opening up of the Buddha's teachings beyond the monastic community and quickly spread to Tibet and China—and from China to Korea, Japan, and Vietnam. A key concept of the mahayana reform was the concept of the *bodhisattva*, a person who has attained enlightenment but who decides to stay in the world and work for the liberation of all beings from *samsara*—the endless round of birth and death, the world of suffering and ignorance and greed. Many mahayana schools of Buddhism recite the four bodhisattva vows, the first of which goes like this: "The many beings are numberless, I vow to save them." At first glance, this intention to save all beings seems puzzling and a bit grandiose. But it is a commitment to the world and an acknowledgement of our connection to all living things. Experiencing this interdependence is at the heart of saving all beings. The bargain is this: We will all wake up together. Try this:

MEDITATION TEN: ABIDING IN THE MOMENT

Sit in your meditation posture and bring your attention to your breathing. Count your exhalations from one to ten and, as your breath gets slower and fuller, think about how your body is right now. Can you accept all of your physical sensations as they are right now in this moment? Now notice the temperature of the air that surrounds you and the smells and sounds of the environment you are sitting in. Accept whatever is in your environment. Now notice how your mind is working right now. Are you agitated or depressed, confused or sluggish? Just notice and accept. As you continue to work on all these elements of acceptance, you will begin to experience joy—which is the simple, peaceful acceptance of your life in this moment. If you lose track of your counting or drift off in distracted thoughts, accept that too. Don't be upset. Notice and accept the distraction, smile to yourself, then return to the meditation.

Now think of someone else in your daily life, someone you do not feel strongly about either in a positive or a negative way. Imagine this person having a good day. Imagine that she can experience this calm joy in the present moment that you have been able to feel. What if she is very happy? Does that affect you? Does it improve the human environment? Image that this person is very happy. Imagine this person benefiting from your experience of joy. Imagine the power of joy.

Christianity, Judaism, and Islam all started out with deep commitments to the common good and to generosity toward others. Buddhism started with an even more basic and existential practice and statement of self-less-ness: there is no abiding self. Buddhist belief also extended the notion of the common good to all beings and all things, living or not. Yet all of these great religions, over the many years of their histories, have gotten caught in the trap of valuing generosity and kindness only to insiders—other Muslims, Buddhists, Jews, or Christians.

The question is, can your practice of mudita bring you to value the fundamentalist chaplain or bigoted fellow inmate in the same way you can value your fellow Buddhists? Are you coming to believe that Buddhist practice is the *only* way to advance spiritually? Is Buddhism right and the other religions wrong? Be very careful! His Holiness the Dalai Lama has often said that religion is not that important—and that organized religions may have historically caused more human troubles than they have healed. Think of the former Yugoslavia; think of Northern Ireland. Think, even, of the many religion-based hate groups in the United States.

If organized religion is not that important, then what *is* important? "A good heart," His Holiness says. Mudita is one way to that good heart.

ABODE FOUR: EQUANIMITY

The English word "equanimity" (our translation of the Pali *upekkha*) comes from the same Latin root as the word "equal" and means the practice of treating everything equally. We begin to learn how to do this in our meditation; we are told not to make any judgments about the thoughts, feelings, or impulses that come into our minds while we are sitting still. We don't beat ourselves up because we lose count of our breathing or because our thoughts wander. We just return to "one" and resume counting. We try not to say, internally, "This was a good meditation session, but last night's was no good." Each thought is equal. Just notice it and return to counting your breath. We watch our minds in action during meditation; we don't judge.

This internal nonjudgment is the beginning of the practice of equanimity and leads us to broader applications in the confusing world of human interactions. The best example of a person practicing equanimity that I can think of was a mentor of mine who was the chairman of a university academic department. This man always said hello and stopped to talk with the building janitor, with the clerks in his department offices, with the man who delivered his mail. He treated all these "support personnel"—as well as his department's graduate students (the lowest of the low in any academic pecking order)—with the same dignity and attention that he gave to his professors. He knew who was having financial problems; he knew the names of his secretary's children and whose kids had just started school or just graduated. He knew who had a sick parent and what that parent's name was. His whole behavior with those around him was in marked contrast to that of his professors—who wandered the halls without saying hello to anyone. They were lucky to remember their own names, let alone the name of some janitorial employee. My mentor's interest in everyone shows one way that the "equal" of equanimity can be put into action.

Another example of equanimity in the prison setting comes from Arturo Esquel, who practices Buddhism at the Pelican Bay Prison in Northern California.

> Many inmates tend to act aggressively toward people who walk a spiritual path, and now that I've given up the gang life-style, there is the strong possibility that I will be attacked, including with weapons. I pray that I can accept whatever abuse I receive from my precious other sentient beings and be able to look upon them with great compassion and love.
>
> This, of course, includes the people I used to see as my enemies: snitches, rivals, child molesters, and the rest. It is clear to me now that these people, for whom I've held so much hate in my heart, only want to have happiness and to avoid suffering, just like me. It is senseless to me now to harbor bad feelings for them or to wish them even the tiniest harm; may I only help them.[2]

Esquel says he came to realize that "if I truly wanted to make others happy I would have to stop labeling people friends and enemies, which is what my gang activities had been based on. I realized that I had to develop compassion for every living being, not just my friends." [3]

Perhaps the most important and basic way to begin the practice of equanimity is by trying to practice equanimity of thought. Notice first. Look at the labeling you do. Investigate what thoughts come automatically to mind when you think of a certain person or type of person. What are the cars in the train of thought that come automatically behind a word like "black" or "white" or "women" or "queer."

Well-meaning people often think that they are free of prejudices, yet this is almost certainly never true, at least in regard to certain habitual, negative thoughts. Everyone (except for the rarest and most saintly among us) has automatic thoughts connected with certain people-related words. Begin to notice what your automatic thoughts are. Learn what categories of people can set you off: cops? lawyers? Latinos? Asians? whites, snitches?

Ohio inmate Gunaratna Sarika talks about how habitual, negative thoughts can be changed by sitting still: "Practice has given me a sense of compassion and with it, a real sense of responsibility for both myself and for others. Before beginning practice I was a real racist and sexist and homophobe—all of that. Now I find I am more accepting, more open, not judging others all the time like I used to." [4]

The practice of equanimity can start in the realm of thought and move to the actions that follow from practicing those new thoughts. The reverse can also be true—practicing new behaviors can help change habitual thoughts. "Fake it till you make it" is a cliché in many twelve-step circles. Act "as if" you cared about listening to someone you think is boring or stupid. Aitken Roshi once talked about just being decent to others, no matter what our feelings are about them. When a student then asked if this wasn't dishonest or hypocritical, Roshi answered, "It is no more dishonest to practice decency than it is to practice zazen. Zazen is the practice of harmony at the source of responsibility. Being decent is simply the practice of harmony in a wider context." [5] Try practicing concern for another inmate who doesn't get visitors. Pretend you care, and you may actually start to care. If *you* don't have visitors, can you be happy when someone else does? Try. Or just start by saying "good morning" to everyone equally, whether you like a person or not. Just try.

Insight meditation, called *vipassana* in Pali, is a mahayana school that focuses on the meditative analysis of thoughts and emotions. This analysis leads us to a realization of the true nature of our experience in the world. Here is a variation on an insight meditation practice intended to cultivate equanimity:

MEDITATION ELEVEN: NOT PLAYING FAVORITES
Bring your attention to your breathing as you settle into your meditation posture. Count your exhalations from one to ten for a few minutes to settle your breathing. Now do a mental inventory of the people you have regular contact with each day. Review the look of their faces or the sound of their voices. Don't play favorites, visualize everyone you routinely come in contact with. Notice how some of the people in your review provoke negative feelings; others you feel neutral about; and still others you like or feel drawn to. Just notice these automatic feelings attached to each of the people in your daily life. Now go back through your list and, after you visualize each person, think something like, "I want you to be safe, to be healthy, to be happy, and to have the opportunity to awaken." That's all. Do this for each person, no matter what emotions you have about him or her. Try thinking the phrases with equal sincerity for each person. When you have finished your list, think of yourself and say the same formula mentally. Do this exercise each day until you begin to experience a true equality of good intentions for each of your fellow buddhas.

Hang in there. None of this is easy. Prisons are very adversarial environments with enemies, real and imagined, everywhere. Grievances spawn even more recriminations. One of the biggest games in any prison system is the attempt to compromise or get one-up on the staff and administration. Prisoners who learn the law inside—who become jailhouse lawyers—sometimes end up focusing all of their energy on assertions of inmate rights to the detriment of their own growth in compassion. All prisons are in need of reform and improvement. And sometimes litigation is the only way to obtain that needed reform. Except for a few family members and a few volunteers, prisoners have no political constituency on their side. The private prison corporations and ambitious law-and-order politicians are a much stronger interest group than prisoners and their families.

But the endless litigation and grievance procedures would be greatly diminished if all sides could understand the need for peace and mutual respect inside the prison system. This may sound like naive, unrealistic thinking, but it is not as outlandish as it may appear to be. Both prisoners and dharma volunteers working inside have repeatedly related how negative attitudes have been changed over time by the exercise of the skills we learn from the four abodes: not judging; patience; not trying to be one-up all the time; not comparing; and not ignoring the needs, fears, or joys of others.

Yet real structural barriers to the encouragement of love, compassion, joy, and equanimity certainly exist in prisons. Guards are trained not to share anything personal with inmates for fear of being compromised. The macho attitudes of many prisoners make any behavior other than assertiveness and aggression seem like weakness. Inmates are encouraged to divide along racial, ethnic, religious, and sexual-preference lines—and to distrust anyone in another camp. Prison gossip encourages more hatred. The prevalence of these barriers may seem very discouraging, like meditating in a field of dead bodies, as Fleet Maull says, or, as in Albert Camus's haunting image, being the only doctor in a country hit by plague.

Part of our practice becomes the effort to break down this me-versus-them attitude—whether the *them* is the court system, the custodial staff, or prisoners of other races or religions. Peace can only happen when we stop thinking of others as the enemy—or, even more radically, when we stop thinking of them as *other* altogether.

Prisoners who have trouble settling into meditation because of strong enemy issues can repeat meditations eight through eleven over and over again until the results start to be felt. Although some forms of meditation may take precedence on a day-to-day basis, these four practices may be returned to whenever daily life offers conflict with other people. More metta-style practices may be found in some of the books listed at the end of this book. Experiment.

This type of meditation work is not meant to be a shallow, "have a nice day" activity. It is difficult work for difficult circumstances. Many Tibetan monks, for instance, have used this kind of meditation work to help them endure imprisonment and torture by the Chinese. Ribur Rinpoche and Palden Gyatso are two examples of Buddhist practitioners who were able to use compassion practice to transform acute suffering into joy—despite the cruelties of their jailers. [6]

None of this practice is easy, yet none of it is optional for the Buddhist inmate. These meditations are practice, which means they are never finished, never fully perfected. Just day by day, we try our best. Jarvis Masters, writing from San Quentin's death row, sums up this quality well: "It is so difficult to integrate my meditation practice with all the suffering here. In trying to live a life that reflects the Buddha's ways, I fail continuously! I know so little! I'm just hanging in there with my meditation. Practice is my best companion." [7]

NOTES CHAPTER FIVE
The epigraph is from H. H. Tenzin Gyatso, The Fourteenth Dalai Lama, in Bo Lozoff, *We're All Doing Time: A Guide to Getting Free* (Durham, N.C.: Human Kindness Foundation, 1995), vii.

1. Arturo Esquel, "Searching for a Way to Leave No One Behind: the Transformation of a Mexican Gangster," *Mandala*, Soquel, Calif.: FPMT, November-December 1997, 46-7.
2. Ibid. 43.
3. Gunaratna Sarika, personal communication, 1997.
4. Robert Aitken, *The Gateless Barrier: The Wu-Men Kuan* (San Francisco: North Point Press, 1990), 224.
5. See Palden Gyatso, *The Autobiography of a Tibetan Monk* (New York: Grove Press, 2000).
6. Jarvis Jay Masters, *Finding Freedom: Writings from Death Row* (Junction City, Calif.: Padma Publishing, 1997), 121.

Outside-In:
Guidelines for Dharma Groups Working Inside

One thing these students needed to appreciate before they began their work with the inmates was that they weren't bringing anything into the prison. Everything needed was already there; wisdom and compassion were already there. Where does wisdom come from? Each one of those inmates in his zazen was manifesting the enlightened life just as we were at the monastery.
—John Daido Loori

In Hawaii, in the late 1980s and early 1990s, there was a prison meditation program staffed by volunteers from several local sanghas. One of the volunteers recounts his first experience meeting with this prison group.

> Our group of volunteers was not very together. Some meditation leaders would allow anyone into the weekly group just to keep the numbers up and feel like the program was succeeding. They'd let guys sleep during the session; the inmates could chat and come and go as they wished.
>
> The first time I led a session, one of the older men came in and started throwing small pieces of hard candy to everyone around the room, including me. I knew the prison rules did not allow exchange of anything in reli-

gious or educational meetings. No one is supposed to even give another person a piece of string, but I didn't say anything. Then, just as I was getting ready to ring the bell to start meditation, I saw this older guy take a baggy out of his sock and pass it to the guy next to him, who quickly put it in his back pocket. I just happened to be looking in their direction and I saw the whole thing very clearly. I was so flustered I just went ahead and rang the bell to start the meditation session—just to give myself time to think.[1]

This real-life dilemma gives us a good example of the kinds of situations that volunteer meditation instructors may face in a prison setting. If you were in his place, what would you have done after the meditation period was over? Prison rules required that he summon a guard immediately. Violating these rules might end the meditation program.

First, a digression: All prisons have flourishing underground economies in which food, drugs, pornography, and weapons change hands constantly. The inmate entrepreneurs who run these supply networks are always on the lookout for opportunities or locations in which their transactions can take place. New classes or programs that are under the direction of volunteer outsiders are almost always tested as possible times and places where these transactions can be carried out. The group of Hawaii Buddhists who had goodheartedly, but naively, let inmates do whatever they wanted in meditation class had ended up creating opportunities for the exchange of contraband. Since U.S. Buddhist groups first started responding to the needs of prisons, dilemmas like this have been played out over and over, with each group left to learn its own lessons by trial and error.

How did our informant in this example solve his problem? After the meditation period, he took the two men out of the room and confronted them with what he had witnessed. "They denied it, of course, and the guy who received the baggy lied, saying he had nothing on him."

Not wanting to escalate the confrontation, the volunteer brought the two back into the room and told the entire group what had happened. He reminded them of the rules and said that these rules would be fully enforced in the meditation class—no passing anything, whether it was candy, a piece of thread, or a baggy of methamphetamine. The two inmates involved were asked not to return, and they did not. Although he is no longer doing prison work, and despite the anxieties of his first experiences, this volunteer says he hopes to return to prison dharma work when he can. "I don't care if I have only one or two guys in the group; it seems worth it to them, and to me, to have this kind of contact."[2] But why is it worth it?

> It is quite literally true that people who want to work with prisoners need to have their heads examined. What the Jesuits developed into a fine art—the thorough examination of conscience—needs to take place before someone begins to do dharma work in prisons. Are you lonely, bored, or unhappy? If so, get to work and find out what's wrong, but don't take up prison volunteer work because you need a pen pal or because you are unhappy and need someone around who is less fortunate or less free than you are.

There are several reasons for this advice. One is that all of us have needs that get met in our paid or volunteer work, but your own needs for affiliation, healing, friendship, or love should be focused on your community in the world and on relations in your own sangha. The second reason for this caution is that once you do find out how to be happier and get your own needs met, you may then move on—leaving the needs of inmates to be looked after by someone else, or, in many cases, by no one at all. Consistency over time is a big but missing factor in many dharma groups' prison efforts.

After these cautions have been considered, it is important to emphasize how fulfilling prison work can be. Buddhist teachers interviewed for this book emphasized over and over how much this work has benefited their own spiritual development. Joan Halifax, a Zen teacher in New Mexico, and Venerable Robina Courtin, a teacher of Tibetan Buddhism in California, both testify to how inspiring inmate students can be— students who must practice despite the many obstacles in their environment. This commitment has the effect of renewing the volunteers' own commitment to practice. Sincere inmates are also very quick to express their gratitude to anyone on the outside who makes time to volunteer inside.

Helping with prison sanghas or meditation classes is a commitment not to be undertaken lightly. I would suggest that anyone contemplating this work should think in terms of at least a three-year commitment. In this way, you will be forced to evaluate the importance of what you are considering doing, and you will also be refining your own motivation before making the commitment. Sanghas should evaluate if their organizations are mature enough to commit to such programs. Sanghas should look carefully at the commitment and the "practice maturity" of the volunteers available—and at how volunteers may be replaced if they move on or drop out of the work.

Even if the local sangha has no structured program, individuals can work on their own by responding to correspondence referred by national or regional Buddhist organizations. But even this seemingly small commitment to write to one prisoner can sometimes mean involvement in a long-term, though long-distance, human interaction.

"BEING THERE" PRACTICE

Some volunteer duties do not involve direct contact or protracted correspondence with inmates. For those interested—but unsure of a three-year commitment—it may be better to help by assisting with office work or hustling for book and money donations to help with the sangha's prison work.

Deborah Barrett, a teacher at Newport Mesa Zen Center in California, emphasizes the importance of long-term commitment whatever the format of the work: letter, phone, or in person.

> One of the things we've found is the importance of persever-
> ance. The practice is: Be there, be there, be there. And you
> can't just say that the whole sangha will do a prison program,
> you have to have two or three people who will be there every
> week. It can't be a new person every week. Even after several
> years [at the Donovan Federal Penitentiary], we still some-
> times have trouble getting in. The paperwork will screw up, or
> they tell us they're in lock-down. I just think of it as a kind of
> bowing practice. You always have to kow-tow to the
> gatekeepers. If you can't do that, you shouldn't work in
> prisons. I still consider it a practice—even if you prepare and
> drive all that way and don't get in, just being there when you
> said you would is your practice. Then you have to look at why
> you were disappointed or angry. What were the emotional
> goodies you wanted? This is *Not-Getting-In* practice.[3]

Barrett also suggests roles for other members of the sangha who can't
make a long-term commitment to prison work. As long as two or three
sangha members are available who are known to prison staff and inmates, then additional sangha members can come as they are able. "Especially in institutions with lots of lifers," she adds, "it's a way they can
meet new people and keep up with what's going on in the world outside."

Lama Yontan Gonpa, of the Padma Ling Center in Spokane, Washington, works with volunteers from his sangha at the Geiger County
Correction Center. "Most of the volunteers," he says, "are prepared by
virtue of their dharma practice. We're dealing with people in a spiritual
dimension, and the prison itself is the training program for volunteers."
He adds that Buddhist practitioners are tolerated at that particular prison
only by virtue of the U.S. Constitution. "If it weren't for that," he says,
"we wouldn't get through the front door." [4]

Reverend Ratnakaruna Kusala, a Buddhist monk who works with

juveniles in the Los Angeles Detention Center, says that staff attitudes in juvenile facilities tend to be a little different than in their adult counterparts. "They still operate from a rehabilitation point of view, so if they see teaching meditation as giving the kids new skills, then they will support the program." Kusala says he tries to operate with the juveniles from this practical point of view. "After I give an introductory talk about Buddhism, I ask how many want to become Buddhists. No one raises their hand. But then I ask how many want to reduce their suffering and all the hands go up. These kids live with very high anxiety levels because they don't know what's going to happen to them."[5]

LETTERS AND PHONE CALLS

Prison dharma work often starts in a haphazard way. In most cases, a dharma center receives a letter from a prisoner asking for help in setting up a meditation group or requesting individual visitation. Sometimes an inmate wants written materials or someone to write to. Often the fate of these letters depends on who happens to be in the office that day. Sometimes they are answered conscientiously; other times they are ignored. Prisoners can often cite the number of letters they have sent to religious groups that have gone unacknowledged.

Letters are very important to prisoners. Many people in the free world have lost the art of personal correspondence with friends. Phone calls and email are so easy and convenient that most of us write only the occasional business letter in our workplace. But mail call in a prison is a loaded emotional moment, even for the most hardened of lifetime cons. Getting a letter is knowing that someone remembers you, someone knows you are alive and wants to talk to you. The structure of prisons is deliberately intended to emphasize to each resident how much of a nonperson he or she is. Letters and visits are among the few things that counteract this numbing and dehumanizing force of "correctional" institutions.

Too many inmates know the experience of the gradual drifting away of friends and relatives as they go on with their outside lives; the prisoner, who is so much out of sight, gradually slips out of mind. Too many volunteers take up the commitment of writing or visiting, only to let the commitment drop when they lose interest or when other matters become more pressing. These lapses of commitment only make things more difficult for inmates—thus, the importance of a minimum three-year commitment, which avoids at least one of the seemingly small emotional disappointments that add up in an inmate's life.

Most of my work with prisoners has been by phone and letter. From this experience, I can offer a number of things to keep in mind for those who are working with inmates in this way. The first letter to an inmate should contain a factual introduction saying what your prison and/or dharma experience is and should give a brief description of your daily life. You may want to use a post-office box or your dharma center's mailing address for this correspondence. Be sure to ask in the first letter what the mailing rules are for that institution. Sometimes you may send an inmate stamps for her or his reply; in other institutions you may only be allowed to send prestamped envelopes. Sometimes mailing books or magazines is allowed, but many institutions want such materials sent directly from bookstores or publishers. Some prisons merely require a "Religious Materials" stamp on the outside of packages containing such publications, but sometimes these must be sent directly to the chaplain. I also suggest you send a photo with your first letter. Photos are very important to inmates and are often used to decorate their cells. The image helps describe you and says that someone is out there, someone is in contact.

It is best, to view your correspondence with an inmate as letters between two dharma friends, rather than as some kind of meditation instruction or teaching relationship. Most of my correspondence has to do with what each of us has been reading lately and with the events of our daily lives. Sharing at a deep psychological or spiritual level may eventually occur, but this is not necessarily the case with most correspondence.

There are some things to be careful about. Inmates who are less interested in practice may attempt to sexualize the contact (whether the outside letter writer is male or female), and these attempts should be redirected as quickly and simply as possible. For example: "I'm not interested in pursuing further discussions in the style of your last letter. If you want to continue the correspondence, please let's limit ourselves to what two fellow practitioners might discuss, without further sexual material." If your request is not followed, discontinue the correspondence, or ask someone else to take it over if you feel the inmate has some genuine desire for dharma, but can't get over an imagined infatuation.

Sometimes you will be asked for money. I discuss this issue as item 10 in the list of guidelines given later in this chapter. Sometimes you will be asked to contact or carry messages to friends or family members. These requests are best redirected and discouraged.

If I receive a letter from a prison correspondent and I know I don't have time to answer right away, I send a reply by postcard saying exactly that: I've received your letter and I'll write back as soon as I can. The gift shop at one of the museums in Honolulu has postcards of Buddhist images in its collection. I usually buy a bunch of these to send as they can then serve as dharma images for inmates' living spaces—and they are much appreciated.

Try to decide before starting a correspondence if you are willing to accept phone calls from inmate friends. First of all, phone calls may not be comfortable for you, and second, they can involve expense. The inmate may also be assigned a phone time that you will need to accommodate. One inmate I used to talk with on the phone asked his ex-wife to send me money each month for phone calls to him. The amount was more than was needed, so I used the contribution to subsidize other callers who couldn't help with the cost.

Most prisons now have contracts with phone companies to provide expensive collect phone service for inmates. A prisoner must phone the person outside, who hears a recording identifying the call as coming from a prison; then that person must accept the charges—often something like five dollars for the first minute and seventy cents to one dollar for each additional minute. Institutions in some states have been sued by prisoners' families over these costs, and more prison administrations need to be sued for these outlandish charges. This is another example of institutions taking advantage of prisoners' families and friends.

THE WHOLE OF BUDDHISM

When a sangha is considering doing prison work, the sangha's teacher or leadership needs to insure that volunteers have a solid, broad-based knowledge of Buddhism beyond their own particular sect or lineage. Volunteers should have a basic acquaintance with the principles of Zen, Theravada, Chinese syncretic, Tibetan, and Pure Land teachings and practices. For the next few decades, at least, the volunteer is likely to be the only Buddhist representative in a particular institution. Thinking that the way his or her own particular dharma group bows, chants, or does meditation is universal—and that any variation in style is wrong—is not helpful. The Twin Rivers Corrections Center in Washington state has monthly meetings with volunteers from three different traditions: Soto and Rinzai (both Zen streams) and a Shambhala Tibetan tradition.

The Angulimala organization, in Great Britain, has had long experience in advocating for Buddhist chaplains inside British prisons. "In our opinion, instruction in meditation and the leading of meditation sessions is the most important part of a chaplain's work. So far as doctrine goes, the relating of the Four Noble Truths, the Eightfold Path and the Five Precepts to the way of meditation is the chief requirement, together with the development of loving-kindness and compassion." [6]

Many U.S. prisons have "ethnic Buddhists"—Chinese, Korean, Vietnamese, or Thai—among their inmates, who may be used to a temple life that focuses on certain Buddhist holidays. Sometimes the celebration of these holidays is what these inmates want most from a Buddhist volunteer or chaplain. And sometimes outside workers have never heard of these holidays. This is another reason why westerners need to educate themselves in all the streams of Buddhism. The western-trained dharma volunteer can seek out ethnic teachers to assist with Asian inmates. If visitations are not a possibility, at least the American volunteer can seek out expertise on ceremonies and practices to meet the needs of this Asian minority in the U.S. prison population. A good resource for this kind of information may be found in John Snelling's *The Buddhist Handbook,* which is listed at the end of this book.

GETTING A PROGRAM STARTED

If an inmate writes requesting instruction or visitation to a prison, the sangha is often faced with the task of trying to respond helpfully while having no one in the group who has any experience working with prison systems. Thus, with the exception of a few national organizations that have formed, each sangha has been left to learn, by trial and error, its own hard lessons. Volunteers need to be level-headed and patient. The best motivation for volunteers is just a sense of sharing the results of an experiment (meditation and mindfulness) that has gone well in their own lives. From one day to another, prison work can be difficult or delightful. For the volunteer's own ego, it should be nothing special. Yet the work is important, especially for those who live inside. In the long term, it is the important work of helping self-scrutiny and compassion to flourish within the bleak walls and wired fences of our prisons.

The first step is to get two or three experienced sangha members together to evaluate the situation and the sangha's resources. One of the first questions might be: Is there an expressed need for this work? Have any inmates asked for instruction or visitation? If not, why would a prison administration be interested in letting you in? The other initial choice that must be made is whether to work through a prison chaplaincy to present a defined dharma program or to work through the institution's educational or social services department to present a more secular, stress-reduction-oriented meditation instruction program. This choice should be determined by the needs of those making the request, as well as by an assessment as to which part of the prison bureaucratic structure is the most open and accessible.

There is a Catch-22 here. Most prisons have a rule against proselytizing, and they also frequently have a minimum number for how many inmates must make a request before an outside worker from any denomination is allowed in. In Ohio, for instance, this number is five. If one inmate wants inside meditation instruction, he risk's breaking the no-recruitment regulation if he tries to get four others to join in his request. (Some institutions have regulations forbidding the recruitment of inmates from one religious group into another. Although such rules may have some justification in preventing religious haranguing or the browbeating of inmates, these rules often originated at the behest of existing chaplains who want their turf to remain unchallenged by "alien" religions.)

Some prisons also have a regulation that to receive visitation or services from a religious group, the inmate must have been a member of that religion prior to incarceration. Because interest in Buddhist training often originates from the circumstances of prison itself—such as being left alone with one's mind or undertaking extensive reading and study—inmates are often unable to fulfill this requirement.

GETTING IN

If there exists a real need, the next question is, Who can commit themselves to several years of this work? These volunteers don't have to be teachers or priests, but they should at least be experienced practitioners who can be trusted to give basic meditation instruction to any newcomer—inside or out. Volunteers should meet with the sangha's teacher or director to examine their motives and discuss what needs to be done. The next task is to contact the chaplaincy or volunteer department of the prison from which the request came.

Before a first meeting, dharma groups should be prepared to answer questions about the credibility of their organizations, their track records with other projects, and some basics about Buddhism. It is best to develop a written proposal detailing how you will spend your time inside. For example, a sangha's proposed outline could look something like this:

DHARMA MEETING FORMAT
Total time: One hour thirty minutes

1. Introductions: ten minutes
Brief meditation instruction is given for newcomers.
2. Dharma talk or reading: fifteen minutes
Video or audiotapes may be used.

3. Sitting meditation: twenty-five minutes
4. Walking meditation: ten minutes
5. Precepts or sutra recital: ten minutes
6. Discussion time: fifteen minutes
Discussion may focus on the dharma material presented, issues brought up during meditation time, or questions inmates have regarding precepts.
7. Three refuges or other brief recital: five minutes

If the sangha prefers to present a more generic, secular meditation program, a one-hour session emphasizing stress reduction might look like this:

STRESS REDUCTION CLASS FORMAT
Total time: one hour
1. Introductions: ten minutes
An explanation of the goals of the group and of the activities for this session.
2. Reading or audio/video presentation: twenty minutes
These media activities focus on information about stress, mental health, self-improvement, or general contemplative ideas.
3. Meditation, yoga, or other experiential activity: ten minutes
4. Discussion: twenty minutes
Focus on the experiential exercise or on ideas presented in the media activity. Emphasis is on the practical application of infor mation to prison daily routine.

BEGINNING
If you pass the first hurdles and gain access to a facility, you will probably be asked to attend an orientation session. Almost all prisons now have orientation programs for outside volunteers. These are important to attend, not only because you have to complete them before being allowed

to work inside, but also because you can become aware of the attitudes of the staff and administration of that particular jurisdiction. Waiting for the orientation may often take time. Pay close attention at the orientation. You will need to become an expert in the rules and procedures of the particular institution—and you will need to follow them precisely so as not to jeopardize the sangha's activities inside.

During the orientation, notice how negative or positive the instructors are about outside volunteers who want to work inside. Prison employees often see volunteers as hopelessly naive "do-gooders." Often these orientations are harsh depictions of prison life and inmate attitudes that encourage the outsider to trust nothing at all in their interactions with inmates. In my experience, guards and other prison personnel sometimes think that they are the only ones who are tough enough not to get conned, who are hardened enough by experience not to get involved emotionally. Remember that emotional involvement between staff and inmates is nearly always equated in the inside world with a compromise of security. This can sometimes be true but is never automatically so.

The first few sessions within the prison will be important. As mentioned earlier, this is the time when inmates with hidden agendas will show up to test the new scene. There will also be those who are mildly curious, as well as others who will turn into genuine dharma students. It is important for the facilitators to remind everyone of the rules before starting the program. During times of meditation, if the inmates are seated facing the wall, the instructors should sit so as to be able to observe the inmates; to simplify matters, everyone could sit facing the center of the room. Whatever the configuration, volunteers need to create an environment that is not conducive to the passing of contraband and that allows the volunteers to be aware of the inmates' posture, restlessness, or other problems during meditation.

Volunteers must also be flexible with their agendas. If, for instance, you had planned to do walking meditation and then find that you are assigned a tiny room, you need to be ready to alter your program at a moment's notice. Remember, too, that most of your problems will show up in the first few sessions, as you are tested by inmates and guards alike. Mair Honan, of the True Heart Sangha in Maine, notes that a volunteer received troubling, anonymous calls for the first several months of the sangha's involvement at one of Maine's state prisons. Fortunately, the suspected inmate caller stopped attending the dharma group after several months and the calls stopped. But Honan is undeterred by these difficulties. One inmate told her: "If you did nothing but showed us how to be with our breath, you'd be changing our lives." [7]

One teacher was faced with an agonizing quandary when a prisoner he was visiting told him about his plans to attack one of the guards. The rules required that any outside volunteer must report inmates' threats of self-harm or harm to others. The teacher did inform the administration; the student saw the teacher's action as betrayal and ended the visits. But that particular teacher would never have been allowed to see any other prisoner in that system had he not complied with the rules.

Sister Helen Prejean is a Catholic nun who has worked as a spiritual advisor to death-row inmates in Louisiana for many years. In her now-famous book, *Dead Man Walking*, she gives an account of her confrontation with a warden who was about to bar her from his prison. She was able to tell him, truthfully, that she had been asked to violate prison rules by one of her counselees, but that she had refused. This strict compliance with prison regulations is what eventually saved her ministry inside when it was under threat by the warden and by a priest of her own church who was the institutional chaplain. So complying with the rules that surround your prison work has to be your number-one priority, especially as programs are getting started.

Some Guidelines for Prison Volunteers

Here is a list of some principles to keep in mind when a sangha or an individual decides to volunteer inside.

1. Think about the commitment carefully—whether it is just keeping up an individual correspondence or beginning regularly scheduled

visitations to a group inside. Continuity and followup are very important. Use the reading list provided at the end of this book to educate yourself. Talk to other dharma groups who have active prison programs.

2. Become an expert in the rules that govern the institution you are going to work with. Attend the institutional orientations. Don't expect people to trust you or to be helpful until you have achieved a nonthreatening profile within the institution. There are no absolute rights of visitation that you, or the inmate, may appeal to. All correspondence and visitation is at the discretion of the institution. Know that as soon as you become an expert in the rules of a specific prison, these rules may be changed. If you wish to send reading materials to inmates, make sure you know the institution's rules about mailed materials.

3. Try to meet and befriend the existing institutional chaplains. They are gatekeepers who are capable of great assistance if they are on your side—or of unrelenting sabotage if they view you as the enemy. Sometimes chaplains must be the ones to receive and approve written religious materials for inmates.

4. No matter how much you might identify with an inmate, never assist her or him in breaking any of the rules. The most frequent request is to take written messages in or out. Explain to the inmate that you would be jeopardizing the whole program if you go along with his or her request.

5. It is not your business to know what brought any inmate into prison. Even among inmates themselves, it is against protocol to ask what someone's crime was. If you feel you need to know an inmate's crime, then maybe you shouldn't do prison work. Very often, inmates volunteer this information after they have known you for awhile.

6. Personal visitations with inmate dharma groups should be well

structured and have little free-form "sharing," especially at first. This structure—emphasizing sitting and walking meditation, chanting and liturgy—will weed out those who just want to get out of their cells for awhile, or who want a new social structure to play ego games with.

7. Be honest in explaining to inside groups what your own experience is—or lack of it. Be willing to say, "I don't know." Ask inmates what inside slang words mean when they use them. Don't pretend to have street sophistication you don't have. Be careful about the use of religious or Buddhist jargon. Explain foreign or unusual terms if you use them.

8. You may be asked to write letters for inmates to the parole or pardon boards that govern their release dates and conditions. Some inmates will attend all sorts of groups just to collect such letters. For this reason, a policy of no letters might be useful. However, if you do decide that you are willing to write such letters, you should limit your comments to the inmates' attendance and behavior while in your sessions. Don't try to predict future behavior or to assess an individual's motivations.

9. Inmates who practice meditation sometimes get fixated on the need for the physical accoutrements of Buddhist practice: zafus, fish drums, bells, incense, Buddha images, robes, rosaries, etc. Depending on the regulations of the particular prison, these accessories may or may not be allowed. The best strategy is not to get caught up in the grievance process over these issues. The outline of a footprint can serve as a Buddha image—just as it did in the early centuries of Buddhist history. If the group is not allowed a bell, use a clap of the hands to begin and end meditation periods. Sitting benches may be made in the prison shop if sitting cushions are not allowed. And so forth. Many of these material things may gradually be allowed as the facility becomes accustomed to the group or as the group gains the support of the institutional chaplain.

10. Sometimes, especially in correspondence with prisoners, you will be asked for money. You need to make your own decision about these requests, as some inmates are truly indigent and helping them with money would be a genuine kindness. You should reply to such requests with honesty, as in, "I barely make it from month to month myself, so I can't send any money right now." If the sangha is working as a group in an institution, it might be best to have a pooled fund for such requests, with allocations decided by the sangha prison program.

11. Some prisoners will ask you to call family, friends, spouses, boyfriends, or girlfriends for them. This may or may not be against the institution's rules, so volunteers need to be careful about acting as messengers or getting embroiled in the emotions of inmates' outside relationships.

12. Prepare yourself for the practice of patience and for the practice of figuratively bowing to people you do not respect or agree with. Drop any expectations and see what the limits of your compassion and acceptance might be. Prison work will teach you about your own limits as nothing else will.

The following meditation will help you visualize the difficulties that inmates experience trying to practice inside.

MEDITATION TWELVE: SITTING INSIDE

Sit in your accustomed meditation posture and bring your attention to your breathing. Count your breaths for awhile as they begin to slow and as your muscles begin to relax. Imagine a sudden change in how other people view you. Imagine that everyone you have known now condemns and avoids you. Imagine that you have deeply embarrassed your parents and your family. Think of how you no longer have friends of your own choice to spend time with. Imagine a total lack of privacy, where you cannot urinate, shower, or defecate without other eyes on you. Think of your environment as always being confused by metallic noises, shouts, and the constant noise of TVs and radios played too loud. Unpredictable loudspeaker announcements top off the noise level. Imagine cigarette smoke constantly in the air. Imagine counting off the days on a calendar for twenty years—or five, or ten. Think of knowing you might never have freedom again. You are an American version of an untouchable caste. No one trusts you. You trust no one. You may be physically attacked at any time.

Accept all this as you breathe. Are you relaxed? Can you ever be relaxed in such a place? How hard is it to calm your breathing and your thoughts in this imagined context? What emotions most frequently distract your practice?

Welcome to sitting inside.

Now start to experiment with accepting each of these negative conditions one at a time. Acceptance means noting that a thing, a condition, or a thought of a condition exists. Accept the imagined or real noise, the imagined or real fear and alienation. Accept the thoughts that become distractions. Return to your breathing. As your breathing continues, try to incorporate these obstacles into your practice. Notice and accept the noise. Notice and accept the lack of privacy and the absence of friends and family. Do not give up. Experience these things as being as impermanent as your breath.

TAKING REFUGE

By now, a good number of inmates in U.S. prisons have "taken refuge," a ceremony I mentioned in the discussion of the precepts in chapter 4. This ceremony is, in effect, a declaration that one is a Buddhist, and it can be a significant milestone in a practitioner's journey toward awakening. Inmate would-be Buddhists need to contemplate whether they are ready to take this step. Outside volunteers can help talk inmates through this process.

The ceremony varies between traditions but usually involves three core activities. First, the person states publicly that she or he seeks refuge in the three treasures: the Buddha, the dharma, and the sangha. In other words, the initiate identifies with the search of the historical Buddha and with the results of the historical Buddha's search. The person then promises to study and follow these findings, which are called the dharma.

Second, the person taking refuge also makes a commitment to live according to certain precepts, or trainings. Usually, these are the five lay precepts. Sometimes the ten grave precepts are given, which are the five lay precepts plus five more: not to discuss the faults of others, not to praise oneself while abusing others, not to be possessive of the dharma, not to indulge in anger, and not to defame the three treasures. These vows are undertaken within the context of, and with the support of, the Buddhist community, the sangha.

The third element of the refuge ceremony is the taking of a new name, which indicates that the refugee publicly takes on a new identity. Volunteers should be aware that the public nature of refuge brings up several problems, for both inmates and prison administrators. Arrangements for the ceremony are often fraught with difficulties and obstacles connected with the security bureaucracy. Some Christian administrators or chaplains may see the refuge ceremony as a "conversion" and, hence, a loss for their own denominations; this is not usually the case, however, as most inmates who become interested in Buddhism have long ago left their religions of origin.

When refuge ceremonies are allowed, they often have to be held under difficult circumstances. San Quentin's Jarvis Jay Masters had to take refuge, with the Tibetan teacher Chagdud Tulku Rinpoche, during regular visiting hours, through a phone and glass window. A translator and a witness, longtime dharma friend Melody Ermachild Chavis, were with Rinpoche on the visitors' side of the glass.

Other complications arise for inmates committing themselves to the precepts and declaring themselves to be Buddhists. At California's Pelican Bay Prison, inmate Arturo Esquel was worried about taking refuge with Venerable Robina Courtin. He writes that this act would mean a major change of identity and increased risk for him. "Many inmates tend to act aggressively towards people who walk a spiritual path, and now that I've given up my gang life-style, there is the strong possibility that I will be attacked, including with weapons." [8]

Masters thought about similar problems, as he questioned himself about taking the precepts and identifying himself as a religious person within the prison environment. Yet in all cases, the taking of precepts and the self-identification as a Buddhist seem to have helped the practice of those who have made this important commitment, including Arkansas death-row inmate Frankie Parker, who took refuge with Zen priest Kobutsu Malone. For any Buddhist, inside or out, refuge means forming a connection with the long line of buddhas who have followed the historical Buddha, Siddhartha Gautama. There are pitfalls in identification with a religious tradition—pride and hypocrisy are just two of them. But public religious identification can also mean having the help of others in your practice—for example, in keeping the precepts. This help from others is what the idea of sangha is all about; we're friends trying to help each other wake up.

Some Buddhist sects use the refuge formula as a constant devotional tool. "I take refuge in the Buddha. I take refuge in the dharma. I take refuge in the sangha." This is one of the most universal Buddhist prayers, and its constant repetition is often recommended for people who are dying or are in great pain—or for people experiencing great anger.

CLASS, CULTURE, GENDER, AND "HELPING"

It is virtually taboo today to talk honestly about issues of class in the United States—let alone of race. Unlike the British, who have spent centuries absorbed in the topic of class, we in the United States cultivate a public fiction that we are a classless society. We pretend that everyone is equal and that differences in income, education, ethnicity, gender, and geography do not affect our communal life. This is a dangerous untruth.

There are real and divisive class differences in this country, and the prison system is one of the best examples of our hidden class structure in action. Just for starters: How many wealthy, well-educated white men are on death row? Or how many in that demographic profile are lifers? Not many. Both in the inmate population and in the demographic profile of custodial personnel, we find mostly working-class, blue-collar people who do not have any of the advantages of affluence or university education.

The few middle- and upper-class members of inmate populations often come from drug, sex, and white-collar crime convictions. This is because drug and sexual addictions, as well as alcohol-related manslaughters, are fairly democratic in how they are represented in different strata of the population. Even with these exceptions, middle- and upper-middle-class people often receive much more favorable outcomes within the justice system because of the advantages that money can buy—as well as a result of subtle class identification on the part of professionals like lawyers, judges, expert witnesses, and even juries. If they are convicted, they are likely to get shorter sentences or be sent to the so-called country club prisons, where physical facilities are good, regulations are lenient, and educational and recreational programs are still in place.

The reason I raise the class issue in regard to dharma volunteers is that a tremendous gulf often exists between the social worlds of U.S. Buddhist practitioners and those of the inmates they want to serve or the guards who must help these volunteers accomplish their work. While many American Buddhists might live simply and don't have much money, nevertheless most American Buddhists I have known come from middle- to upper-middle-class backgrounds. Most have good educations and are widely read. A good number may even be "trust-fund babies," with secure and generous incomes, or professionals who are very much part of an elite class. Many sanghas in the United States are virtually all white, with perhaps a few Asian-Americans thrown into the mix—mostly because of Buddhism's origins. I remember thinking about an African-American lifer I corresponded with, an active Buddhist, "Good thing he's a lifer, because if he ever came out, he'd realize the sangha that serves his prison is totally white." Perhaps this is an unkind thought, but it is a realistic one.

Women and people in the gay community have been able to form nonsectarian sitting groups to support each other in their Buddhist practice, and some African-American Buddhists are experimenting with the same process. Diversity is certainly a real problem in the U.S. Buddhist community. Two-thirds of the three refuges—Buddha and dharma—may be the same for all Buddhists, but sangha is a more difficult issue. As conditions are now, few people with ethnic or class differences would be comfortable in the white, yuppie ambiance of most American Buddhist centers.

Prisons in the United States are outposts of the general culture of poverty that flourishes out of sight of mainstream America. Within this culture of poverty—which includes all ethnic groups—the rates of addiction, depression, and crime are high. Potentially wide gaps exist between the values and belief systems of most dharma volunteers and the internal maps of the world used by many prisoners. Middle-class people tend to believe their lives are self-determined, whereas people from the culture of poverty tend to see life as something that happens to them, rather than something lived out through individual will.

Another class difference concerns gender role expectations. The roles of men and women may be perceived differently by outside volunteers and by inmates, both male and female, who tend to see these roles more conservatively. There is some controversy in dharma groups about whether women volunteers should work in male institutions or male volunteers in female prisons or jails. The intense same-sex environments of prisons has been lessened somewhat by the increasing presence of women working as guards in male institutions and vice versa, but the issue still remains controversial.

Women entering all-male institutions will always be subject to a certain amount of sexual acting out by male inmates. This behavior can occasionally be overt but most often happens subtly through verbal innuendo or body language. Because of this built-in tension, some dharma groups have a policy of male volunteers for male institutions and female volunteers for female institutions. But there are also many women successfully doing dharma work in male institutions. A good compromise is to have mixed teams. Of course, overt acting out by inmates needs to be dealt with directly and quickly. How an inmate views the opposite sex may be a part of what he or she needs to change. Gender issues will always be an important subtext when working with inmates.

Although male prisoners in the United Stages outnumber female prisoners by roughly a factor of 19 to 1, the stiffening of drug penalties has also increased the total number of women being incarcerated. In 1972, there were 6,269 women sentenced to a year or more in state and federal prisons. In 1995, that number had risen to 59,409—almost a tenfold increase in total female inmates. Yet, aside from some vipassana retreats held for women in the North Seattle Rehabilitation Facility, there seems to be little outreach from sanghas to institutions for women. Vivian Snyder, the vipassana teacher who led a ten-day Seattle retreat for women inmates, describes the experience as "incredibly enriching,"

> because all the students benefited tremendously. There was visible transformation at the end of the retreat. Women who started the course with dulled eyes and great fears left with a much deeper understanding of themselves: They were glowing. We had the same discipline problems as any outside retreats, but these women already deeply understood the first noble truth of suffering. They worked as hard as anyone I've seen. They didn't come with intellectual or philosophical issues to ponder. The women's deeper understanding came from observing the precepts, developing their concentration, and especially from observing their physical sensations with equanimity.
>
> The seven of them had bonded before the course, and had made a kind of pact with each other. They were afraid of what would come up for them. But they were afraid and they were brave at the same time. Lucia Meijer, who is in effect their warden, came in each day and meditated with us, and that was very powerful for them too. They were a very diverse group: two Native Americans, two African-Americans, one Latina, and two Cau-

casians—but they bonded so completely that at the end
they declared themselves "dharma sisters." [9]

With such possibilities for change, it is a shame that women's institutions seem to be getting overlooked. This imbalance of effort needs
close scrutiny.

HOST AND GUEST

The many differences between people outside and inside may accentuate
the dharma volunteers' delusions about doing good for another—in the
form of someone more downtrodden, less educated, and certainly less
free than themselves. Host and guest, helper and helped, male and female, incarcerated and free—these are just a few of the difficult dual-
isms that intrude into dharma programs in prisons.

The best way to work through these dynamics is for outside volunteers to think of inmates as full members of their own sanghas and to
visualize them as participating in day-to-day sangha functions. The
volunteer's role then becomes a more neutral one of encouraging a friend
in practice. Try to visualize the inside meditator when he or she is released. Would he fit in the local sangha? How would she be accepted? If
we see problems ahead, perhaps sanghas need to address any issues they
have with including these newly released members. It is time for American Buddhist groups to support the development of sanghas within ethnic and gender minority communities and in communities where the
culture of poverty predominates. Perhaps this is the next necessary step
in Buddhism's historical development in the United States.

Inmates, too, need to de-mythologize the importance of the outside,
as Daido Loori has emphasized. It is helpful if prisoners can see outside
volunteers as fellow Buddhists who share what they can with their peers
on the inside and who, realistically, can do a number of things that insiders cannot.

Prison work may become one of the most important challenges of
U.S. Buddhism—not just to see if U.S. Buddhism can be socially en-

gaged but rather—and more important—to see if it has room for every-one. Too many American sanghas have a "high church" elitist aura that silently excludes those of other classes, ethnicities, or gender orienta-tions. This atmosphere can be so pervasive and subtle that sangha mem-bers, like fish unaware of the water they swim in, rarely see it themselves.

"Helping," in any of its forms, is a potential briarpatch of ego en-tanglements. The twin notions of equanimity and emptiness can assist both helper and helped in relationships that are complicated by power and status differences. Doing the dishes is no better or worse an activity than eating a meal—this is where the practice of equanimity leads us. Both activities may be occasions for the practice of mindfulness. Just so, helping activity should spring forth from the realization of emptiness and no-self—and from the understanding of the interdependence of all things. We all need to get there together. This is the intent of the mahayana vow to save all beings. No thing and no person stands alone. We are all empty of abiding self, even though we still cling to our imagined and cherished egos. The whole world must awaken together.

Assisting others, whether doing the dishes or doing psychotherapy, should be a matter-of-fact imperative in the development of compas-sion, a matter-of-fact effort to insure that all of us get there together. Helping means, above all, "being there" for people, without any expecta-tions of their reactions to our being there—and without attachment to our own needs to feel (or look) good. Actor and Zen student Peter Coy-ote reminds us that the bodhisattva of compassion always says, "After you."

CHAPTER SIX NOTES

The epigraph is from John Daido Loori Roshi, "Lotus in the Fire: Prison, Practice and Freedom," typescript, n.d.

1. This source wishes to be anonymous, personal communication, 1998.
2. Ibid.
3. Deborah Barrett, personal communication, 1997.
4. Lama Yontan Gonpa, personal communication, 1997.
5. Ratnakaruna Kusala, personal communication, 1998.
6. Anonymous, from Angulimala Web site: www.angulimala.org, 1997.
7. Mair Honan, personal communication, 1998.
8. Arturo Esquel, "Searching for a Way to Leave No One Behind: The Transformation Mexican Gangster," *Mandala,* November-December, 1997, 46.
9. Vivian Snyder, personal communication, 1998.

Dying Inside
with Fleet Maull

Birth is an expression complete this moment. Death is an expression complete this moment. They are like winter and spring. You do not call winter the beginning of spring, nor summer the end of spring.

—Eihei Dôgen, 1233 C.E.

What a dying inmate wants most is not to be dying in prison. He or she wants out. A prison death is, for many, the ultimate mark of failure in life. The greatest hope of most terminally ill inmates is to survive their illnesses until they finish their sentences, or to receive a "compassionate release," which happens in only a few cases. They want to be cured or let out to die at home. Inmates on death row, who have been sentenced to be executed, continually hope that their executions will be stayed or their sentences commuted. No inmate wants to die in prison.

Four trends make dying inside a serious issue for all those concerned about the welfare of inmates: First, the sixfold increase in AIDS incidence within state and federal prisons since 1985. Second, the aging of the prison population, as the "baby boomer" demographic bubble moves through the system. Third, the trend toward longer mandatory sentences, like the increasingly popular "determinant," or no-parole, sentence. Last, the dismal and immoral resumption of capital punishment by many U.S. states. To put it simply, many more men and women are dying in U.S. prisons than ever before, and—based on these trends—it seems certain that this will continue into the foreseeable future.

Buddhism, like all religions, is about both living and dying. It places great emphasis on living with awareness of the inevitability of death and on being properly prepared for the actual death event. Both the vipassana (insight) and Tibetan traditions have developed detailed spiritual exercises to help people prepare for death. American Buddhism has also engaged itself in the hospice movement. San Francisco, for example, is home to the San Francisco Zen Center's Zen Hospice Program and the Maitri Hospice, which sprang out of the Hartford Street Zen Center. On the East Coast, Issan House, associated with Roshi Bernie Glassman's Zen tradition, has founded both a residential program and a day program for the terminally ill.

No one will escape death, and yet the circumstances and surroundings of dying can differ markedly from person to person. Prison is probably one of the worst situations in which to die that anyone could imagine—bleak and comfortless and lonely. Prison journalist Wilbert Rideau writes that dying in prison means

> dying away from home, alone, with strangers, in the callous atmosphere of prison, being treated and cared for, more often than not, by an indifferent hand. It's grossly different from dying in the warmth of home, in the bosom of friends and relatives, which eases the sting of death somewhat. There is nothing in the prisoner's world that can soften the finality of death. A longing look out a window reveals a world of guns, curses, and noise as callous as the concrete it's made of. There is no warmth, beauty, or meaning—no last pleasures, touches, joys, words. In prison, there is nothing—you suffer alone and you die alone, feeding the fear and misery of those who must watch you die. [1]

Christian prison chaplain Gary Penton explained to Rideau why this is so in a 1984 interview for *The Angolite*, the award-winning newspaper of the inmates at Louisiana State Penitentiary at Angola. Penton had just performed his first funeral at the facility.

> The fact of death is no major fear or dread or terror for me. That's a natural part of life. But the death where there is nobody to love you, to mourn your passing, no tears, that's sad. Standing at the head of his grave, I found myself identifying with him and those gathered around. I can relate to the pain, the fear. A man who is as much a family man as I, a man who feels the need for human warmth and belonging, I can appreciate the value of family relationships. [His death represents] the fear of not only the inmates but that of every living human, of being alone in life. It's a very human fear. It's just that with the inmate it's worse, more intense, because he doesn't have that much control of his life, his being. Life in prison is much more intense. When you're excited, you're really excited, and when you're depressed, you're really depressed. And your fears are very, very real to you, whether they're real or not; they run that much deeper. Oh, I understand their fear. [2]

THE PRISON HOSPITAL OR INFIRMARY

Fear of dying is a part of the human condition whether we are incarcerated or free. Yet dying in prison is different from dying outside, for many reasons. For instance, terminally ill patients in prison and their families have virtually no choice of primary caregiver, treatment, or medication. Medical and nursing staff are restricted by security procedures and are often given insufficient time to attend to their patients. Protocols for pain management are frequently inconsistent or nonexistent. Many prison staff physicians, afraid of encouraging drug abuse or addiction, are overly conservative in prescribing painkillers, even to dying patients.

Fortunately, these conditions and attitudes are changing somewhat, and pain management has improved in recent years at some of the more progressive state and federal facilities. However, at many institutions the situation remains dismal, and poor attitudes and staff ignorance of new medical developments persist. Budget cuts have created shortages of staff, equipment, and medications. Prison hospital wards are characterized by many limitations and constraints that are unknown in outside clinics or hospitals. Security is always the first priority, more important than any quality-of-care values. Staff morale is often poor, and equipment and supplies may be decades behind the state of the art found in outside facilities.

The attitudes of the patients' primary caregivers—physicians, nurses, and ward correctional officers—vary from benevolence and caring to professional decency to outright indifference or hostility. Staff who wish to give their patients optimal care often risk the resentment and suspicion of their colleagues when they do so. As in traditional hospitals, the great majority of prison hospital nurses are women. In a men's prison, female nurses who spend any more than the minimal time alone with their patients may suffer the suspicions and criticism of correctional officers or her fellow nurses. Unfortunately, demonstrating an attitude of compassion or kindness toward inmate patients is not always conducive to good professional peer relations in the prison setting.

Patients who are weak, feeble, or semiconscious from illness or medication are often preyed upon by inmate hospital workers, or even by their fellow patients. Items of value—like watches, sports shoes, or radios—may frequently disappear as a patient's condition deteriorates. As a patient's illness progresses, those who have seen this happen to others often voice their fears about ending up in that kind of helpless or defenseless condition. Some prison hospital workers even charge patients for the services they are supposed to provide as part of their duties and ignore or do the minimum for patients who will not or cannot pay. It is also common for inmate hospital workers to remove portions of meat, fruit, and desserts from patients' meal trays before delivering them.

Further compromising the nutrition of inmate patients is the tendency for prison food to be of poor quality and served in an unappetizing fashion. The nature of prison food can become a big problem, especially for AIDS patients going through the wasting syndrome and experiencing nutritional compromise. Seriously ill patients often have difficulty eating even food they like, let alone facing the usual prison fare—despite the fact that they know their very lives may depend on eating well.

Prisoners do not have the support systems available to patients who are free, who can get support from family and friends. Those in federal prisons are likely to be far from home, making visits very expensive for loved ones. Visiting rules and access vary widely from state to state and from one institution to another, but, in general, families have very limited access to their loved ones in prison.

When inmates are taken to outside hospitals, they are often kept under guard, and families may not be allowed to visit at all. In fact, families are sometimes not even informed of the locations of their loved ones. When a patient can't get to the prison visiting room because of his or her deteriorated physical condition, ward visits by family members are often limited to only an hour or two and are closely supervised. Children under eighteen years of age are not normally allowed to visit on the ward. Patients may also be isolated from their families because of their own or their families' sense of shame. In some cases of lengthy incarceration, family relations have simply dropped away. Increasing access and improving visitation conditions for family members, significant others, and friends of dying prisoners, is a primary goal of the prison hospice movement. One new prison hospice in Texas has set a truly heartening precedent by allowing twenty-four-hour bedside visitation by the patient's family and friends during an inmate's final days.

Within the prison community itself, patients are often kept on locked wards; they are unable to go to the recreation yards for fresh air, participate in education programs, or go to the prison chapel for religious services—or for just a moment of real silence.

Even in the small world of a prison hospital ward, patients may be further isolated by the debilitating effects of their disease, by language barriers, by the fear of being abused by others, or, in the case of those with AIDS, by the fears that others have about their disease. Although patients in outside hospitals may share some similar constraints, the prison environment of distrust, anger, and hostility intensifies these conditions.

THE SPRINGFIELD PRISON HOSPICE MODEL

The hospice model of palliative care for the dying was first implemented in a prison setting in 1987 at the Medical Center for Federal Prisoners in Springfield, Missouri. The concept has since spread to prisons in California, Florida, Illinois, Louisiana, Maryland, Michigan, Minnesota, Texas, and other states.

The Springfield hospice program model makes use of trained inmate hospice volunteers to provide skilled assistance, companionship, and emotional support to terminally ill prisoners. The inmate volunteers are trained by outside community hospice professionals and institution staff. Volunteers are supervised by the nurses, social workers, and chaplains who make up the hospice team. The hospice team meets weekly to review the status and current needs of each patient, as well as to provide ongoing training, clinical supervision, and support to the inmate volunteers.

The Springfield program is modeled on traditional hospice practice. The patients, physicians, and nurses focus on symptom relief and pain management. If a cure is no longer possible, the primary goals of treatment are comfort and quality of life. The hospice social worker often works with the patient and the case management team in preparing a petition for a compassionate release, though few of these requests are approved. The social worker on the team relates with the patient's family, dealing with a variety of issues that may be of concern. The hospice chaplains and outside religious volunteers provide religious care and pastoral counseling. The inmate hospice volunteers serve in the roles of trusted friends and companions, providing emotional, spiritual, and practical day-to-day living support.

During the course of the patient's illness, the hospice volunteer provides whatever physical or domestic assistance the patient needs; he or she simply tries to "be there" for the patient. Hospice volunteers give moral support and understanding, much as close friends or family members might do. An important part of the volunteer's job is helping the patient deal with the institutionalized callousness and brutality of the prison environment. Volunteers assist patients in communicating their needs to the staff, and they try to help them avoid the angry outbursts and self-defeating conflicts that patients often have with prison hospital staff. Inmate patients often perceive medical staff as the enemy or as the police. Volunteers encourage their patients to express their frustrations to the hospice workers rather than to the medical and nursing staff on whom they must depend for their primary care.

The volunteers also help their patients to explore their own resources, to look for ways to make their daily lives richer and more meaningful. If the patient is willing and able to work on healing any personal or family rifts—or on any other unfinished business—the volunteer helps with that, too.

The onset of the dying process itself—a stage that can last from a few days to a few weeks—changes the focus of the hospice volunteer's work. Caregiving now centers primarily around just two issues: physical pain and fear. At this point, the focus is on keeping patients comfortable and on helping them to face their fears.

If they have not done so before, the time of dying is frequently when patients voice religious or spiritual concerns and make requests for prayer or other pastoral services. When possible, a chaplain or volunteer who shares the same faith as the patient will attend to him or her. Often, though, chaplains and volunteers must step beyond the domain of their personal beliefs to address religious needs and concerns of patients when no one of the patient's own faith is available.

At the same time, all members of the hospice team should be involved in providing spiritual care, which is a larger and more inclusive domain than sectarian religious or pastoral care alone. Pastoral care has to do primarily with specific religious beliefs and practices; whereas spiritual care in the broader sense addresses such basic issues as the ability to find meaning in life, to give and receive love, to feel forgiveness, and to experience hope. Hospice volunteers are trained to be attentive throughout the caregiving process to these spiritual needs in their patients.

Because hospice volunteers in the prison setting often become the sole emotional and social support for their patients, especially in the latter stages of the dying process, they often become surrogate family members. Thus, a patient's death may put the volunteer through his or her own bereavement and grieving process. Recognizing this issue, volunteers in the Springfield hospice program are encouraged to share their feelings of loss and grief during their weekly hospice supervision and support meetings. The prison chapel also conducts quarterly memorial services to which all prisoners and staff are invited to remember those who have died during the previous three-month period. In this inter-faith service, a friend of the deceased—often the person's hospice volunteer—is invited to light a candle on the altar as prisoners and staff take turns sharing their memories of each prisoner who has died.

THE EMOTIONAL STAGES OF DYING IN PRISON

A prisoner's life is pervaded by the experience of loss: loss of freedom, loss of dignity, loss of former social or professional status, and, most critically, the loss of the supportive environment provided by family and significant others. Many prisoners have experienced the complete disintegration of their families through divorce and have lost visitation rights with their children. Others may have lost all their former wealth, great or small. Simply put, many inmates have lost almost everything that formerly gave meaning to their lives.

Terese Rando, a leading authority on grief and bereavement, defines grief in part as "the reaction to many kinds of loss, not necessarily death alone," and she cites fifteen types of loss experienced by dying patients.[3] All the dramatic losses experienced solely as a result of incarceration are included on her list, indicating that prisoners may have severe grief reactions by virtue of their imprisonment alone. Rando also describes anticipatory grief, or grief for future losses. When a prisoner is told about a life-threatening illness, he or she will grieve, not only for all that has already been lost, but for all that will be lost in death. It is not surprising that terminally ill prisoners experience a profound process of grieving that is compounded by the effects of their incarceration.

Even healthy prisoners commonly experience the five stages of bereavement and coping behavior identified by Elisabeth Kubler-Ross: denial, anger, bargaining, depression, and acceptance.[4] New arrivals, fresh from trial and sentencing, are typically in denial. They simply can't believe that the worst has happened. They are certain that their convictions will be overturned on appeal. They often talk about being back on the streets in a matter of weeks or months, as soon as their lawyers get the papers filed.

As appeals are lost and the reality of doing prison time sets in, denial turns to anger and then to depression. Bargaining with good behavior and program involvement for the hope of parole is commonly mixed with underlying hostility toward the system and all those who represent it. The emotional stew that pervades life in prison is a mixture of anger, hostility, and hope (usually unrealistic) for some early reprieve. Though some prisoners do move beyond anger and blame toward a healthy degree of acceptance, self-responsibility, and growth, most inmates remain angry and bitter throughout their time inside.

When a prisoner receives a medical diagnosis of terminal illness on top of the grieving process already begun by incarceration, his or her mental distress can become dangerous. The diagnosis is the last straw, the double whammy; it is like being kicked when you are down. The alternating cycles of hope and fear are already in place, and the terminal diagnosis just intensifies the suffering as each patient goes through the five stages of coping with death.

DENIAL: COPING WITH THE FEAR OF DYING IN PRISON

Patients in the hospice program at Springfield commonly react to their diagnoses with extreme shock, almost immediately followed by withdrawal and depression. Sometimes the patient appears to spin through all of the first four Kubler-Ross stages in a matter of hours or days. But as the initial shock wears off, denial normally emerges as the predominant coping mechanism. Confronted by the likelihood of dying in prison, the patient's initial reaction of denial is perhaps the most useful defense against the onslaught of an overwhelming sense of fear, isolation, hopelessness, failure, and despair.

The denial process for incarcerated patients is complicated by the almost universal belief among inmates that if they could get outside medical care they would not be dying. Therefore, prison hospice patients typically focus on the hope for an early medical or compassionate release, which seems easier than adjusting to the prospect of dying, let alone dying alone in prison. Inmates—who have already been expelled from normal society—see death in prison as the ultimate indictment of a failed life.

Paul, for example, a prisoner in his late forties, was admitted to the hospice program at Springfield in the terminal stages of AIDS. When the hospice volunteer first visited him, he was receiving an intravenous blood plasma supplement for the treatment of AIDS-related anemia; yet he insisted that he was only in the early stages of the illness. Although he claimed that his condition was not very serious, he was also convinced that he would soon receive a compassionate release. He focused all his attention on these two inconsistent beliefs: that he was eligible for early release by reason of a hopelessly terminal prognosis, and that he was in the early stages of the illness—with the additional hope of living until a cure could be discovered for AIDS.

Because early medical releases from prison are usually granted only to those with a terminal illness, many prison patients face this same double bind. Psychologically they need to deny the seriousness of the condition and maintain hope for a cure, while they need simultaneously to acknowledge the seriousness of their illness in order to qualify for early release. A few patients have intentionally accelerated their own deterioration by not eating or by refusing medications, hoping to get a compassionate release and then rebound and seek improved treatment once they are free—a dangerous game of brinkmanship. One such patient died three days after his release, but he did fulfill one burning desire: He did not want to die in prison, and he did not.

ANGER

Scratch the surface a little with just about any prisoner and what you will find is anger. For those in the second stage of coping with dying, this anger borders on rage.

Anger pervades the daily lives of prisoners. They are angry at themselves and at the system that keeps them locked up. As terminally ill patients, prisoners also experience rage over their limited treatment choices and at what they perceive is the substandard medical care provided by their institutions. Whether based on fact or not, this anger is quite real to the patients and is often their only method to express the frustration, hopelessness, and fear that typifies their experiences of daily life. At a certain point, the only choice seems to be between withdrawal into depression or angry lashing out. Anger is sometimes healthier, when it can be directed into positive action, but all too often, anger brings patients into conflict with their primary caregivers, the prison nurses and physicians.

Rando and Kubler-Ross discuss the appropriateness of the terminally ill patient's anger: It is a way of coping with underlying feelings of grief, anxiety, and fear—and it is a perfectly normal reaction to the loss of control and other frustrations inherent in dying in an institution. They stress that caregivers need to be tolerant and understanding, allowing patients to express their anger within reasonable limits. Of course, a fine distinction exists between facilitating the unproductive escalation of aggressive behavior and helping patients move toward what Kubler-Ross calls, "a better acceptance of the final hours." [5]

Unfortunately, what often occurs in the prison hospital—with its atmosphere of distrust and tension—is quite the opposite of what Rando and Kubler-Ross advocate and results in escalating hostility and self-defeating, aggressive behavior. The process of dying should also be the process of peacemaking; instead, patients and staff sometimes use each other as convenient targets for displaced anger. Patients may learn to habitually project and displace their anger onto staff, which delays the process of letting go of anger and moving toward acceptance.

Peter, a prisoner in his early fifties with advanced liver and heart disease, was admitted to the hospice program with a prognosis of less than three months to live. He was convinced that his life could be saved or prolonged if he could just be released to an outside hospital and into the care of free-world physicians. He believed that his prison physician had given up on him, and this belief made him intensely angry. He became extremely demanding and battled with the nurses and other staff, including the inmate nursing attendants. As a result, people avoided him, and he received a minimum of care. This treatment, of course, made him even more angry; during one visit by his hospice volunteer, Peter flew into a rage. He leapt from his wheelchair and hobbled frantically back and forth ranting about his dilemma. With tears streaming down his face, he agonized about the lack of care and attention he was receiving. He died a month later, still angry and bitter, never getting beyond this stage.

BARGAINING AND HOPE

Terminally ill prisoners often bargain actively for early release. Some participate in religious activities; others pursue litigation. Many do both. Although some patients may seem resigned to approaching death, they often want to taste freedom just one more time or be with their families just once as a free man or woman. They sometimes hold onto the hope that, once released, they will get such improved medical care that they will be cured.

The only chance for early release for most patients is deterioration to the point that death appears imminent. Prisoners strive for more time and better health to pursue the legal actions needed for release, but any sign of actual improvement only lessens the chances they might have for approval of compassionate-release petitions. Patients often exhaust themselves in these efforts, becoming angry and bitter about the prospect of dying in prison.

John, a fifty-five-year-old prisoner with lung cancer, was admitted to the hospice program in deep depression shortly after having a court-ordered compassionate release overturned. The prison medical staff had reported to the parole board that he was responding well to chemotherapy. His depression was aggravated by the fact that he had just received news of his father's death. Later, his depression began to lift, and he became more energetic in litigation for his release. He worked to improve his health by paying attention to his nutrition and by becoming more physically active. He began to participate in religious activities, cultivating a relationship with a visiting chaplain of his own faith. But John's anger over the parole board's decision, and the medical staff's complicity in it, never abated, and he remained obsessed with fighting the decision in the courts. He avoided any preparations for death and refused to deal with family conflicts that had arisen during his incarceration.

After about six months of this assertive activity, John gave up on both his litigation efforts and his religious activities. He returned to a state of isolation and depression, became recalcitrant, and exhibited increasingly bizarre behavior. He ate so little that staff and prisoners who knew him well believed that he was deliberately allowing his health to deteriorate so that the parole board would release him. The staff continued to insist that the chemotherapy was working and that John's cancer was in remission. John, on the other hand, insisted that he was in constant pain and was, in fact, dying.

Based on his rapidly deteriorating condition, however, the parole board finally ordered his release. Although fearful he might die during the night, John was coherent and happy the evening before his scheduled freedom early the next morning. According to the report of a friend, John died peacefully in a hospital near his home three days later.

In John's case, as long as he had hope for release, he coped well with his fears that he might die a lonely and shameful prison death, but when he relinquished that hope he became depressed and quickly deteriorated physically. Most prison patients never stop hoping for and regularly express, until the final stages of their dying, the wish for compassionate release.

The most frequently discussed issue among prison hospice volunteers is how to encourage their patients to hope, in general, while still helping them to maintain some degree of realism about the specifics of their situations. As volunteers watch patients and families ride the roller coaster of hope and fear, they often get caught up in the emotional ride themselves. Because such mood swings are exhausting, many prison hospice volunteers have become wary of involving themselves in the process at all. Nevertheless, the bargaining involved in the compassionate-release issue, as unrealistic and futile as it may seem, is of primary concern to the vast majority of terminally ill prisoners and their families—and must be faced.

DEPRESSION

When the inevitability of dying in prison becomes obvious to a patient, hopelessness, despair, and deep depression usually follow. This may be a "reactive depression," brought on by the combination of incarceration, illness, and loss of hope. Or it may be what Kubler-Ross calls a "preparatory depression," which normally occurs in the late stages of the dying process.

Reactive depression often reaches pathological proportions in the prison setting and may seriously endanger the patient's remaining health, actually accelerating the dying process. The stigma and sense of failure associated with dying in prison, the fear of dying alone, and the colorless, depressing physical environment all contribute to dangerous episodes of despair and, in some cases, suicidal behavior. Because prison hospice patients are often in this state of potentially lethal depression when they enter the program, volunteers generally try to engage them in any kind of positive activity that can return some meaning and hope to their lives. Volunteers may also help by advocating with the physician to give antidepressive medications to patients who might benefit from these.

A thirty-seven-year-old man named Roger was admitted to the prison hospice program with advanced AIDS. The hospice volunteer found him in a state of complete despair and isolation. Because of an angry outburst with a guard in which he threw his meal tray to the floor, he was on lock-down status, which meant he had lost television privileges. After this incident, Roger simply quit caring for himself. His room was disordered and dirty; he was unshaven; his hair was long; and his hygiene was poor. But after several weeks of companionship, attention, and encouragement from his volunteer, he began to make a complete turnaround. He cut his hair, started to shave again, and became fastidious about his hygiene and the cleanliness of his room. He also began attending religious services with the volunteer and gained new hope for extending his life and, possibly, returning home.

This situational, reactive kind of depression can quickly be lifted in many cases in which the patient's basic emotional and social needs begin to be met with the help of a volunteer. This is one of the most obvious successes of the prison hospice program. In fact, many patients who were considered to be near death at the time they were referred to the program have made dramatic physical recoveries. Even after leaving the hospice program in improved health, many of these inmate patients have kept up supportive relationships with their volunteers.

Most of the time, however, any elation seen at the stage in which reactive depression is overcome turns out to be short-lived. The dying process will inevitably proceed for most patients. As this process gains momentum, preparatory depression appears. At this point, the volunteer must consciously shift her or his attention to the patient's need to prepare for death. Sadness, letting go, and withdrawal are part of the final adjustment process. As the patient makes this shift, volunteers need to deal with their own anticipatory grief over losing this person in whom they have invested so much caring and friendship.

Tyler, a fifty-year-old man referred to the hospice program in the later stages of AIDS, was very hopeful of receiving a compassionate release. He talked freely with his volunteer, and gradually they established a strong relationship. They often passed evenings together on the prison yard watching softball games. They also attended regular religious services together. They developed a spiritual bond and often prayed together in Tyler's room. One day, without apparent warning, Tyler began to lose interest and vitality. He became withdrawn, depressed, and uncommunicative—to the point of frequently falling asleep during visits from his volunteer. He also began refusing food, became agitated, and paced the halls at night.

The volunteer first thought that something—possibly in Tyler's family—had occurred that he wasn't sharing. The volunteer also wondered if he himself had done or said something to alienate Tyler, although he couldn't imagine what that might be. The volunteer questioned him, but Tyler said that nothing had happened and that there was nothing to talk about. He assured the volunteer that he was at peace with himself and with God. He continued to withdraw physically and emotionally and, within a few weeks, he died. By that time, the volunteer had come to realize that Tyler was simply withdrawing from the relationship as he prepared himself internally for death.

At the memorial service, this volunteer shared his fond memories of the good times they had spent together, enjoying softball games and praying. He also was able to talk about how difficult it had been for him to adjust to Tyler's withdrawal in preparation for death.

FINAL STAGE: ACCEPTANCE

The acceptance stage of dying, described by Kubler-Ross as the last stage in the process, may actually occur very infrequently among terminally ill patients—both inside and outside prison wards. For inmates, the psychological and spiritual work involved in reaching any degree of acceptance is made all the more difficult by the fear and shame that they feel as they anticipate death. If the eventuality of dying is acknowledged at all, some form of bitter resignation is much more common than any degree of acceptance. It is hard for a prison patient, or anyone, to imagine dying in prison as a "good death."

"Realization of the inevitable" may be a better description of this final stage than "acceptance." The patient may never be at peace with death and its losses, but he or she may at least move beyond denial into an acknowledgment of what is: the reality of approaching death. Although some degree of acceptance would certainly be desirable, this sense of realism about death may be a more reasonable and practical goal for patients to achieve, especially in the prison setting.

An even more reasonable approach to working with dying prisoners may be to have no goal at all, to allow them to experience the dying process naturally. Frank Ostaseski suggests as much in an interview about his work as director of the Zen Hospice Program in San Francisco. "I've never had a situation," he says, "in which I couldn't trust the dying process. It's very potent; it does it's own work, just like the birth process does." [6]

These observations are compatible with the experiences of inmate hospice volunteers working with their patients through the final stages of dying. In many cases, volunteers observe that the drama of anger, shame, and bitterness about dying in prison disappears as death actually approaches. The patient's greatest wish as death approaches is commonly that she or he not be left alone. The presence of the hospice volunteer, as a friend and surrogate family member, provides comfort and reassurance throughout the final days.

Scott, a twenty-eight-year-old former heroin addict and bank robber, was admitted to the hospice program with advanced AIDS. Throughout his illness, he had fought hard to regain his health and had great hope that a cure would be found for AIDS. His focus was on survival, and he refused to discuss the possibility of dying—though he clearly thought about it. He was often angry about his illness, about his imprisonment, and about his fate in life. He railed against his predicament and fought for life almost to the very end.

But during the last few days of his life, he calmed down considerably and appeared at times to be in a different world, often conversing with persons not physically present. He seemed immersed in a world of memories or, perhaps, in glimpses of the other side of death. Several hours before dying, he told a fellow prisoner and longtime friend, "I don't think I'm going to make it." That was it, just a simple acknowledgment of the fact of death.

WHAT YOU CAN DO

The following section is addressed to Buddhist prisoners interested in including some form of service (*dana*, generosity or giving) to other inmates as a part of spiritual practice. This section is also directed to outside Buddhist prison volunteers or teachers interested in dealing with terminal-care issues. And, finally, this section is meant for terminally ill and death-row Buddhist inmates.

The Springfield experience is important because it came out of the determination of one inmate to make a change for the better. This robust young man, a former martial arts instructor, found himself living on a prison medical ward, confined to a wheelchair and facing an uncertain future. Paralyzed from the waist down as a result of gunshot wounds suffered during his arrest, he knew neither whether he would ever walk again nor how he would survive the lengthy sentence he had received. Life had brought him to a place of total "not knowing."

Seeing the suffering around him in the ward, this prisoner felt called to service. He befriended an AIDS patient and then a cancer patient—both of whom were dying far from friends and family. He stayed with his two friends through the final stages of their illnesses and deaths. In doing so, he discovered two things: that there was a great need for this kind of caring outreach, and that in doing this work he himself had received profound internal rewards. Caring for his prison brothers in this way gave new value to his own life and gave him the self-respect that comes from being a giver rather than a taker. He experienced this work as a blessing—a life-changing, transformative experience.

One of the first obstacles he had to overcome in bringing his hospice idea to fruition was the negativity he found in his fellow prisoners. "I was shocked, hurt, and angered by the pain, fear, and sadness I witnessed, by the loneliness and lack of support, by what I recognized as apparent apathy to the needs of these poor unfortunates by some of the staff, and by the fact that even other inmates would not encourage my efforts to initiate this program. They felt it could not be accomplished, especially by an inmate. I was angry at the helplessness I felt." [7]

Resistance from the administration was also a problem at first, but he was not to be dissuaded. He got the support of key staff sponsors and, with their help, campaigned hard for the program. After a year of persistent effort, a pilot project was finally approved. In November 1997, outside community hospice professionals were allowed to conduct the first-ever hospice training inside a prison in the United States. Ten inmate volunteers were trained.

The same inmate talks about the spiritual and emotional benefits he found in hospice service:

> I am a paraplegic. I was shot during my apprehension in 1986; but I have come to realize that I am not helpless to affect change, regardless of my physical limitations or environment. It was an affirmation I needed for the sake of my self-esteem. I feel better about myself. I feel good about being able to make a difference. There are a lot of patients that have benefited and were able to replace fear with hope. I feel their joy. . . . A lot of things come into perspective when you are around a lot of death. For me, my values have changed. It's like I was sleeping for a long while, and now I've finally woken. . . . I have forgiven most of my anger. I don't like the burden of having to carry it. I realize people hurt others out of fear and pain. I have forgiven myself for not understanding this sooner, and for putting myself through it all. . . . I can't change the past. I would if I could, only to alleviate the trouble and pain I've caused people I care about—and others affected by my actions.[8]

The Springfield hospice program began with the inspiration and hard work of one inmate reaching out to his fellow prisoners. More than fourteen years later, this highly successful program—now a national model for prison hospices—is still serving the needs of terminally ill prisoners.

The Springfield hospice has provided comfort, companionship, and a measure of dignity to over 400 men who would otherwise have suffered their dying in lonely isolation, with only their fear, anger, and hopelessness to keep them company. More than twenty additional U.S. prison hospice programs have been modeled on the Springfield program bringing the same dignity, compassion, and hope to hundreds, perhaps thousands more. All this is a result of one inmate's commitment to service.

AN OPPORTUNITY TO SERVE

The point of this example is to underline the fact that prison time does not have to be "down time" or time to merely endure. The days, months, and years of a sentence may be used to transform oneself and others through generosity and service. Hospice programs are starting up at more and more prisons around the country. Volunteers are also needed in AIDS buddy programs and HIV/AIDS peer counseling projects. Prisoners who live in facilities that house terminally ill patients can participate in existing programs or help start new ones where they are needed. HIV/AIDS awareness and peer counseling programs are needed at all prisons.

Dorothy Day, an activist for the poor and cofounder of the Catholic Worker movement, frequently spoke about "the call to service." She spoke of this as a sacred calling in that the very best in us is called forth in response to the suffering of others. There is a place in the human heart that, when unblocked, can spontaneously respond to the anguish of others. In traditional Buddhist language, we use terms like *metta* (lovingkindness), *bodhichitta* (awakened heart), and *karuna* (compassion) to describe this universal and inherent human capacity. This openness of spirit is our ideal relationship to others and it includes the sufferings and joys of all beings, including ourselves.

Many of us, because we have felt hurt or have been betrayed in one way or another, have closed off access to this awakened heart energy, building an almost impenetrable wall around our feelings. Out of fear and distrust, we operate mostly from the point of view of emotional survival rather than emotional skill or competence. Those of us who have committed crimes were helped to do so by our lack of ability to feel for our victims. Empathy and compassion have to be taught. Crying infants want milk, without apologies for annoying others with their screams; as we grow up, parents and others must teach us to notice the needs of others. Meditation practice and service to others are the two most important teaching methods in the spiritual world. Through these methods, we can awaken to the world beyond our own survival-oriented egos. Like the paraplegic prisoner at the Springfield prison hospital, we will begin to find ourselves responding to the sacred call to service that has guided the lives of people like Dorothy Day.

For the Buddhist volunteer, with nontheistic beliefs, it can be confusing when patients of other faiths ask you to pray with or for them. But the Buddhist emphasis on openness and inclusiveness is actually an ideal foundation for such interfaith ministry. Although it is always good to bring in a chaplain or volunteer who shares the patient's faith, there are times when this is not possible. As volunteers, we need to be prepared to fully support the spirituality of our inmate patients without fear and with complete acceptance.

The flip side of this issue is the problem of proselytizing that goes on in prisons. If a terminally ill Buddhist inmate is being subjected to this kind of evangelizing—either by prison chaplains, outside religious volunteers, or other inmates—the volunteer can be of help by finding peaceful ways to protect him or her from this kind of aggressive religious behavior.

Buddhist Practices for Volunteers

The Buddhist practices of mindful awareness and insight meditation uniquely prepare the volunteer to sit mindfully in silence with the patient—often the ministry most called for in the care of the dying. Hospice work has often been referred to as "a ministry of presence." Both the ability to be fully present with someone who is suffering and the quality of our presence are strengthened by the daily practice of meditation. Here are two simple meditative practices from the Tibetan tradition that you can do at a dying patient's bedside.

MEDITATION THIRTEEN:
EXPANDED AWARENESS AND SHARED BREATHING

First, simply sit at the bedside and do your accustomed meditation practice, while expanding awareness to be attentive, not only to your own posture and breathing, but to the patient's as well. Cultivate a quiet, stable, relaxed mind in yourself. This will always put the patient more at ease. Expanding your own awareness to include your patient's presence will train your attentiveness to the patient's state of being and needs.

Second, having established this kind of attentive presence, begin a practice called "co-meditation" or "shared breathing." Synchronize your breathing with the patient's breathing cycle and rhythm. If the patient gives his or her permission to be touched, you may also place one hand lightly on the patient's hand, arm, chest, or shoulder—as a way of making another point of connection.

This practice might be embarrassing or scary at first, especially if the patient is breathing rapidly or erratically. You don't have to match the frequency of breathing when the patient's respiration is very rapid or erratic; you can just be very aware of the patient's breathing, whatever the speed. The point is to be aware of his or her breathing and to maintain your own meditative awareness and calm presence. In this way, your efforts will have a very calming and reassuring effect on the person.

When patients are conscious and able to communicate, always explain these practices and ask their permission to do them. You could just say that you know a relaxation technique that is very soothing and calming and ask if he or she would be willing to try it with you. When patients are not conscious, speak to them anyway as if they can hear you—they probably can— and explain simply what you are doing.

When the patient appears fearful and anxious, continue the co-breathing practice but ask the patient to listen to you while you begin to extend your breath out, voicing the very natural and universal sound of letting go: "aaaaaaahhhhh . . . , " on each exhale. Most often, patients will begin to slow their breathing to match the sound of your outbreath, bringing on a more relaxed state and helping them to let go. You can actually assist someone through his or her final letting go in this way, right to the final exhalation: "aaaaaaahhhhh. . . ."

A third practice, from the Tibetan tradition, is called *tonglen,* exchanging self for other through the medium of breath. You can do this practice by yourself at the patient's bedside or on your own at any time. Very clear instructions for doing tonglen appear in Sogyal Rinpoche's book, *The Tibetan Book of Living and Dying,* a bestseller in the hospice community.

MEDITATION FOURTEEN: EXCHANGE OF BREATH

Tonglen is a meditation practice in which, on each in-breath, you imagine that you are taking in another person's (in this case your patient's) suffering, pain, fear, and negative karma. Let yourself visualize this person's suffering and distress in the form of a thick, black, hot, and heavy smoke that fills up your body and dissolves into your heart, destroying all the ego-clinging at the very core of your being, thus purifying your negative karma and revealing your inherent Buddha nature—your basic goodness. Then, on the exhalation, breathe out your own inherent goodness, healthiness, peace, joy, and sanity in the form of a cool, white, healing light, which you imagine extending out and enveloping the patient, purifying all his or her negative karmas.

Actually imagine that you are breathing in and out through all your pores as well as through your nose and mouth. Before ending a session of tonglen, it is good to gradually expand the practice to include other people and then all beings. It is also a good idea to do five or ten minutes of basic mindfulness-of-breathing meditation both before and after tonglen.

It is common for new practitioners to wonder if they could be harmed or become sick as a result of doing tonglen practice. Tonglen has been one of the most highly regarded practices in Tibetan Buddhism for over a thousand years, so it is quite clear that it helps rather than harms the practitioner. Sogyal Rinpoche has said that the only thing tonglen *could* harm is the grasping ego. [9]

END-OF-LIFE ISSUES WITH THE BUDDHIST PATIENT

If you are working with a Buddhist patient, he or she may have questions regarding various end-of-life issues, like the use of pain medication, the handling of the body after death, and the disposition of the remains—whether to bury or cremate.

In general, there is no universal Buddhist teaching on these issues. However, the patient may belong to a Buddhist tradition or ethnic community that has prescribed traditions regarding the handling of death. In such cases, following the guidelines of that tradition may be very important to the patient. As a volunteer, you may be able to assist the patient in getting an institution to honor such prescribed religious practices. Following are some general guiding principles that may be helpful.

First, although it is certainly good for a Buddhist practitioner—especially someone who has experience with meditation or other mindfulness practices—to die with as much awareness as possible, this doesn't mean that he or she can't receive pain medication. A person suffering great pain will not have anything like an ideal meditative awareness at the time of dying—in fact, quite the opposite is likely. The problem in prisons has more often been a lack of medications rather than overmedication. It is just as important for the dying person to be comfortable and at ease as it is to be aware. Maybe more so. With or without pain medication, disease and physiological processes make many dying people appear relatively unconscious during the final days and hours of their lives. What is most important is that people realize they are approaching death and that they can draw near to the end of their lives with as little fear and as much calm as possible.

Second, regarding the handling of the body after death, it is generally recommended in Buddhist tradition that the death scene itself remain as peaceful and undisturbed as possible and that the body also remain as undisturbed as possible. In some traditions, three days is considered the ideal time for the body and surroundings to remain undisturbed. But this isn't possible in most medical or correctional settings. Medical personnel will need to check vital signs and pronounce the person dead. Corrections personnel will need to photograph the body and take fingerprints. The body will then be cleaned and placed in a body bag for transport, usually to an outside funeral home.

As a fellow prisoner, you may not be able to have much impact on this process, but anything you can do to maintain a peaceful environment before, during, and after death will be very helpful. If nothing else, you can remain peaceful yourself, using your meditation as a grounding for your actions. Any overly aggressive advocacy with the staff can sometimes add more chaos than peace to the situation. Practicing basic meditation in the presence of a dying person is one of the most effective ways to support him or her in the dying process, as meditation helps to create a stable and peaceful environment for everyone involved.

Third, there are no immutable rules determining disposition of the remains. Cremation is the disposition of choice in most Buddhist traditions but is not universal or absolutely required. Cremation is a stark reminder of impermanence and is an act of nonclinging. But this decision is clearly up to the wishes of the person who dies. You can be helpful in assisting a Buddhist prisoner to sort out these issues. It may be important for the person to make his or her wishes known to family and for family members to achieve some comfort with those decisions, especially if the family follows a different religious tradition and prefers another method of disposition.

Embalming may be another issue. From a traditional Buddhist perspective, it is probably best that a body not be embalmed. However, state laws almost always require embalming if the body is to be transported. The best way to avoid embalming is for the prisoner to elect for local cremation.

If a Buddhist wants his or her body to remain relatively undisturbed for the traditional three days after death, he or she may request that the local funeral home wait that amount of time before cremation or embalming for transport. During that time, the body will be kept refrigerated in the funeral home or the prison morgue.

Given the realities of prison life and security procedures, you just do the best you can with these issues. The most important thing is for the patient to be comfortable with his or her decision and to make that decision known to the prison authorities and to the family in writing. It is counterproductive to allow these issues, and the prison restrictions that impinge on them, to add fear or anger to the inmate's dying process.

Buddhist inmates may want to do some simple ceremony after the death of a fellow inmate, whether that person practiced meditation or not. In the Buddhist traditions of China and Tibet, a service is held three days after the person's death, then seven days after, and then again on the forty-ninth day after the death. Annual remembrance ceremonies, on the calendar day of the person's death, may then be held for as long as is practical. A ceremony may be as simple as offering incense or dedicating one's usual meditation or chanting practice. In many Buddhist traditions, a photo or a piece of paper with the deceased's name in calligraphy is placed on the altar, where it remains for the first forty-nine days of mourning. Many temples have special chapels with altars containing these photos, plaques, or urns with cremation ashes. A simple ceremony may be held in a prison setting by doing sitting meditation together, then chanting a sutra, then asking each person who wishes to speak about the deceased to do so briefly. The ceremony may end with a chanted gatha dedicating the zazen and the service to the memory of the individual.

Some prison medical facilities allow beside visits by approved outside religious volunteers in the infirmary or on the medical ward. If you or your sangha are already involved in providing meditation classes, literature, correspondence, or other types of support to a prison or jail, you can approach the prison chaplains with an offer to provide pastoral visitation and counseling to seriously ill prisoners. As a prelude to this offer, it would be a good idea for those involved to complete a hospice training course—usually a two-day, twenty-hour program.

If you are already trained in hospice work, and live close to a prison or jail that houses seriously ill inmates, you might consider helping to train inmate hospice volunteers or assisting the institution with the expertise to begin an inside hospice program. An excellent resource for information and practical support is the National Prison Hospice Association; contact information may be found at the end of this book.

An individual sangha might also consider getting together with sanghas of other Buddhist traditions in a given geographical area and starting an intergroup prison outreach, similar to those undertaken by the Hospitals and Institutions intergroup committees of Alcoholics Anonymous. Existing Buddhist intersangha councils in some urban areas might want to consider a similar approach concerning death and dying issues, as well as to insure, by coordination of resources, that basic dharma instruction is available in all the local jails and prisons where inmates may want it.

Inmates sometimes die by violence. Whether by their own hands as suicides, or as the victims of aggression from guards or other inmates, such fatalities often have profound negative effects on the prison community—all the more reason for inside dharma groups to facilitate discussion in regular prison sangha meetings and to encourage memorial services that allow all inmates concerned to express their sorrow and bewilderment. Even if the inmate who died was never interested in meditation, the group can still hold a simple ceremony, such as the one described, as funerals and memorial services serve the needs of survivors more than those of the deceased.

Most prisoners have at one time or another thought of suicide. When another inmate actually does take his or her own life, this act has a profound effect on the morale of the institution. When a prisoner dies at the hands of another, the priority of the inmate Buddhist community should be peacemaking. Such deaths often inflame ethnic, gang, or staff-versus-inmate tensions. Rumors run like unchecked wildfires through the prison population. These can be teachable moments, crucial times for an inside sangha to review the teachings about harmful speech and nonviolence. A "dharma gate" may open at such times and show the way toward compassion and peacemaking.

FOR INMATES FACING DEATH

Terminally ill Buddhist inmates, or those facing execution, can remember the words of the great Zen ancestor Bodhidharma, who said, so simply, "Life and death are important. Don't suffer them in vain." [10]

Facing the inevitability of dying is something we all must do at some point. But facing the prospect of dying in prison is a challenge only you, who are going through it, can fully discover how to endure. It may be no comfort to say so, but the fact is that inmates on death row enjoy a certain advantage over other practitioners: They have some forewarning about the actual time and circumstances of their deaths. This means that there is both the time and the motivation to prepare to face death with as much awareness, resolution, acceptance, and fearlessness as possible. From the Buddhist perspective, the time remaining can be of tremendous value in preparing for death.

For terminally ill inmates, acceptance does not mean that they should sink into some kind of suicidal resignation. Of course they should fight for their lives—whether in a medical or a legal battle, it is a natural instinct and a right to attempt to survive. But at the same time, as Buddhists, we are called to appreciate every moment of our lives as a further opportunity to attain enlightenment for ourselves and to benefit others. So the trick is to balance fighting for life with preparing realistically for the certainty of death. Fighting for your life is a form of clinging, which needs to be balanced by the practice of nonattachment to self that meditation offers. In other words, do your best, whether this means working on legal procedures or maintaining health in the face of a potentially terminal illness. Then, as much as possible, let go of any concern, fear, or hope about the outcome of these legal or medical efforts.

Whether you believe in life after death, rebirth (the Buddhist term), reincarnation, or even nothing after death, there is a good argument for careful preparation. Buddhist scholar Robert Thurman quotes the French philosopher Pascal to remind us of the air-tight logic of preparing for our own death. "For even the most diehard materialist, Pascal's famous 'wager' is still compelling: If we become nothing after death, we will not be there to regret having prepared for something. But if we are something after death, and we have not prepared at all, or are badly prepared, then we will long feel bitter, painful regret. So we have everything to lose by not preparing, and nothing to gain; we have everything to gain by preparing, and nothing to lose." [11]

The two most critical factors in our dying process, according to Buddhist teaching, are the stability of our mind at the time of death and the ability to let go of this bodily form and all attachments to this life. Properly practiced, the basic mindfulness-awareness meditation discipline shared by most Buddhist traditions is an ideal preparation for dying. The practice cultivates stability of mental awareness and the emotional ability to let go. Sitting upright with a straight back has proven to be an ideal posture for meditation; but if you are no longer able to sit up straight, you can do the practice lying down or in any other position that is stable and comfortable.

It is important to note that meditation is not a replacement for pain medications. The idea is not to see how much pain you can endure but, rather, how meditative attention can become part of a pain-management strategy. Medications should ideally be at a high enough level to relieve pain while still allowing enough awareness to meditate.

DEATH BY EXECUTION

The most troubling cause of death in prisons is death by execution. In the United States, between 1967 and 1976, there was, in effect, a moratorium on executions. But since 1976, when the Supreme Court ruled that the states could resume capital punishment under new, supposedly more just, sentencing guidelines, 697 executions have taken place, as of January 2001. According to the Death Penalty Information Center, by 1997, the use of killing as a punishment for certain offenses had increased to more than 74 executions per year. In that same year, the state of Texas executed 37 inmates, accounting for more than half of the national total. Our level of governmental killing is higher than that of any other industrialized country—most of which abandoned the death penalty many years ago. The resumption of executions in the United States seems to be a part of the blood lust and vengefulness that characterizes public sentiment about crime and criminals. Capital punishment is a symptom of the high levels of violence the United States has permitted in all areas of its national life.

Melody Ermachild Chavis, a member of the Buddhist Peace Fellowship and a professional investigator in death-row cases, says that in the federal prison system the number of executions began to increase during the George Bush, Sr., administration, but it was "with the Clinton administration that the list of federal offenses for which the death penalty can be sought has increased dramatically. The same administration also pushed through laws to 'streamline' the appeals process. This means that everything is speeded up and it makes it even more likely that innocence can be by-passed as a mere annoyance in the rush to get people executed."[12]

The arguments of execution proponents are made from three points of view: justice, deterrence, and economics. But the arguments do not hold up when the facts are checked out carefully. For instance, according to the Sentencing Project (see contact information at the end of this book), a life-imprisonment sentence is cheaper to carry out (at about $600,000) than the death penalty, which requires two jury trials—one for a verdict and one for sentencing—and often includes years of expensive legal appeals. Most states house inmates who are sentenced to death in special "death rows," which are much more costly to run than general-population prison units. The estimated cost of carrying out a death penalty, from indictment through execution, is more than three million dollars. Just paying for the death-penalty appeals process for one inmate in 1997 cost the state of Oregon $546,000. These costs came after the original trial and do not include the actual death-row custodial costs.

Neither the police nor criminologists believe that the death penalty is an important deterrence to crime. A 1995 survey of police chiefs found that they ranked the following as more important for crime prevention: reducing drug addiction, creating more jobs, simplified court procedures, longer sentences, more officers on the streets, and reducing the number of guns. The chiefs ranked the death penalty after all these other measures.

Some crime statistical studies have compared the murder rates in states that use the death penalty to those that do not and found a much higher rate of murder per 100,000 of the population in death-penalty states. Crime statisticians have also noted increases in murders just after public executions have been carried out. The death penalty is also notoriously biased racially and economically; there is no question that it is applied unfairly. For instance, according to the Death Penalty Information Center, of the 102 federal cases since 1988 in which the U.S. attorney general has authorized the pursuit of the death penalty, 80 percent of the defendants were of minority races. Also, 80 percent of the executions carried out in 1997 were in the southern states. In the United States, rich white men who live in the northern states apparently need not worry about the death penalty.

The other argument against government executions, of course, is the possibility that innocent people will be killed. The Death Penalty Information Center announced in 1997 that sixty-nine death-row inmates had been released since 1973. Many of these releases have been the result of the advent of DNA testing in the late 1980s, which led to the exoneration of about fifty already-convicted inmates. But despite the proven risk of killing the innocent, Congress passed the so-called habeas corpus reform in 1996 to limit the appeals possibilities of death-row inmates. By enacting this law, conservatives hoped to "streamline" and speed up the average ten-year death-row stay.

In 1996, because of the race/class unfairness issue and because of the procedural problems involved, the American Bar Association called for a new moratorium on the death penalty in the United States. But for Buddhists, the real reason for opposition to the death penalty stems not so much from any of these arguments as from the clear and simple teaching of the first precept, which opposes killing in any of its forms.

In the United States, the death penalty seems only one more element in a culture of violence in which government executions both confirm and contribute to the evil they purportedly punish. As the Friends Committee to Abolish the Death Penalty, a Quaker group, has said on its buttons and bumper stickers, "Why do we kill people who kill people to show that killing people is wrong?"

Death row is where U.S. prisoners wait for their executions. The two most well known Buddhists on death row in recent years have been Jarvis Masters, who remains living on the San Quentin, California, death row, and Frankie Parker, who was executed by the state of Arkansas in August 1996. As noted in previous chapters, Masters has written a book, *Finding Freedom: Writings from Death Row*. In it, he gives the following description of the shifting emotional states he experiences in death row's special mental world—a world of life while waiting for death.

> I don't fear death most of the time, but what I do fear all the time is how I'm going to die. It has been decreed that I be put in a chamber that will gas the breath out of me, while people watch, write, and sketch me strapped in a chair, fighting for my life. It will be society's statement that something inhuman has been executed. When I think about the fact that society, a nation, has sentenced me to death, all I can do is turn inside myself, to the place in my heart that wants so desperately to feel human, still connected to this world, as if I have a purpose. But then the next day, a prisoner will ask me to write a letter for him because he doesn't know how to write, and I'll say sure, grateful to him for giving me another reason to be at peace.[13]

In California, where Masters resides, almost five hundred inmates await execution. The numbers vary from state to state, but what is important is the unique and netherworldly existence that death-row prisoners endure. Death row's uniquely lonely and isolated environment, and its constant reminders of approaching death, make meditation and other spiritual practices seem more urgent and meaningful than they might to inmates in the general populations of our prisons.

THE DEATH OF FRANKIE PARKER

Arkansas death-row inmate Frankie Parker had a great change of life through the practice and study of Buddhism. His story has become an important milestone in the history of Buddhist involvement in capital punishment issues in the United States. Parker was first exposed to Buddhist thought while in solitary confinement. Knowing it was his right to have a copy of the Bible, even in "the hole," Parker shouted to the guards that he wanted one. When a cynical corrections officer threw him a copy of the *Dhammapada* instead, he picked it up and started reading his first Buddhist text. It was a moment that set him on a course that would change his life and the lives of many others.

In 1984, while under the influence of cocaine, Parker had murdered his estranged wife's parents and seriously injured her. He had felt that his in-laws were responsible for the breakup of his marriage. The Arkansas courts sentenced him to death by lethal injection, and he eventually became the twelfth person executed in Arkansas since that state resumed executions in 1990.

Parker's history as a Buddhist brings up some very core issues about "conversion" that will always haunt prison practitioners. The most fundamental question is: Has this inmate made an authentic, deep change of thinking and behavior? Or does the conversion have other, more pathological motivations? Before Parker picked up the *Dhammapada*, guards and fellow inmates knew him to be troubled, troublesome, and dangerous. He was often thrown in the hole for disciplinary infractions. But after he began to practice meditation, to study Buddhist texts, and to correspond with Buddhists on the outside, his behavior started to change. Sandi Formica, who corresponded with and visited Parker from her sangha in Little Rock, says that the guards in the Bible Belt prison were so curious about Parker's change of behavior that they wanted to know more. "Now almost every time I go to the prison, a guard or someone will want to know about Buddhism. I feel like a church lady sometimes," she says. [14]

Although the guards and his Buddhist visitors were very impressed with Parker's sincerity and with the transformation of his behavior, others were skeptical. Parker's mother, Janie, who was doubtful of his conversion at first, later told the *New York Times:* "I thought it might be a fake at first because so many of them get jailhouse religion, but the longer I talked to him, the more I realized he was into it." But his ex-wife was never convinced. Pam Warren Bratcher thought his "conversion" was just a way to manipulate others and to gain his own release from the death sentence. She told her hometown newspaper, the Forrest City *Times,* "Jesus forgave the thief on the cross next to him, but the thief still had to pay for his crime with his life. It wasn't just forgotten."

Yet Parker's intense practice and study of Buddhism was a source of inspiration for the many American Buddhists who were to come in contact with him. In addition to contact with the Little Rock Ecumenical Buddhist Society sangha, Parker visited, corresponded, or talked on the phone with Thich Nhat Hanh, Kobutsu Malone, Robert Aitken Roshi, Lama Tharchin, and many other Buddhist leaders. Even His Holiness the Dalai Lama wrote to Arkansas Governor Jim Guy Tucker on Parker's behalf. His cause drew many American Buddhists into an intense campaign to save his life with a gubernatorial stay of execution. And this campaign served to educate many in the U.S. Buddhist community about the issue of capital punishment. The traditional Buddhist precepts charge us all to revere life in all its forms. Many Buddhists have now learned to be more aware of, and more firmly in opposition to, all state-sponsored killings—whether the victims are Buddhists or not. "Engaged" Buddhists are now starting to network with, and learn from, the longstanding anti-capital-punishment groups that Quakers and Catholics, among others, have organized over the years.

Although the Arkansas authorities were unmoved by the campaign and allowed his execution to proceed, perhaps it was Parker's karma to educate a whole generation of sangha members about the death penalty. His greatest legacy might be that many more U.S. Buddhists now actively work to oppose death by government in our own country. His last message—written August 8, 1996, on a lined yellow legal pad two hours before he was to die—hints at this outcome to his killing and at his hopes that other prisoners may be touched by the light of compassion.

> For eight years I have worked on kindling a small light of compassion out of deep remorse for the pain I have caused. This little light is now extinguished. I pray that through some small miracle, this light may be re-kindled in the heart of another who experiences deep and profound remorse. Saul of Tarsus was one such spirit. I pray that others who have committed heinous crimes may find that the small light that I have kindled is an inspiration and spread the flame of compassion to illuminate the entire universe, so that all beings may realize the fundamental compassionate nature that resides in all of us.
>
> Thank you, Jusan Fudo Si-Fu Frankie Parker [15]

In the witness room at the Tucker, Arkansas, prison, about a dozen Buddhists chanted the refuges: "I take refuge in the Buddha, I take refuge in the dharma, I take refuge in the sangha." This refuge chant is a classic Buddhist accompaniment to the final stages of dying, and Parker himself was chanting it as he lay strapped to a hospital gurney and received the lethal injection that took three minutes to end his life at 9:04pm.

Notes Chapter 7

Coauthor of this chapter, Fleet W. Maull, M.A., was an inmate in the federal prison system from 1985 to 1999. He is now living in Colorado and working as U.S. Director of the Peacemaker Community, as well as Executive Director of Prison Dharma Network, which he founded. He has counseled dying prisoners at the U.S. Medical Center for Federal Prisoners since the hospice program started there in 1988. He has written extensively for hospice and Buddhist publications and, in 1991, founded the National Prison Hospice Association.

1. Wilbert Rideau, "Dying in Prison," in Wilbert Rideau and Ron Wikberg, *Life Sentences: Rage and Survival Behind Bars* (New York: Random House, 1992), 171.

2. Ibid. 177.

3. Terese Rando, *Grief, Dying, and Death: Clinical Interventions for Care Givers* (Champagne, Il.: Research Press, 1984), 15.

4. Elisabeth Kubler-Ross, *On Death and Dying* (New York: Collier/MacMillan, 1969).

5. Ibid. 54.

6. "Living with the Dying: An Interview with Frank Ostaseski," Interview by Kim Addonizio, *The Sun,* August 1989, 2-4.

7. Anonymous, unpublished notes, n.d.

8. Ibid.

9. Sogyal Rinpoche, *The Tibetan Book of Living and Dying* (New York: Harper SanFrancisco, 1992), 207.

10. Bodhidharma, *The Zen Teachings of Bodhidharma*, trans. Red Pine (San Francisco: North Point Press, 1987), 13.

11. Robert Thurman, "What is Death?" *Tricycle*, Fall 1997, 28.

12. Melody Ermachild Chavis, personal communication, 1997.

13. Jarvis Jay Masters, *Finding Freedom: Writings from Death Row* (Junction City, Calif.: Padma Publishing, 1997), 97.

14. Sandi Formica, handwritten letter to Robert Aitken, from the files of Robert Aitken Roshi, 1996.

Good Time, Hard Time, Real Time

The way the self arrays itself is the form of the entire world. See each thing in this entire world as a moment in time. Things do not hinder one another, just as moments do not hinder one another. The way-seeking mind arises in this moment. A way-seeking moment arises in this mind. It is the same with practice and with attaining the way. Thus the self setting itself out in array sees itself. This is the understanding that the self is time.

—Eihei Dôgen

As Bo Lozoff has pointed out, we are all doing time, whether we practice inside or outside. But time becomes a special preoccupation for prisoners. Sentences are given in terms of time: five, ten, or twenty years. All prison sentences are noted by markers of time: date of parole board eligibility, date of hearing, date of release, date of completion of parole or probation. The prisoner, in our common cultural image, steadily marks off the days, and these days are the currency of society's punishment.

But the days and hours and minutes are not just the punishment; they can also be the raw material of our waking up. The complicated quote from Dôgen that begins this chapter is worth looking at in detail, because it contains the expression of the thirteenth-century meditation master's conviction that time and self—and, therefore, time and practice—are completely intertwined. For instance, "The way-seeking mind arises in this moment. A way-seeking moment arises in this mind." The two sentences do not cancel each other out. Bodies are in time, minds are in time, prison sentences are in time. There is no self without time. There is no practice except in time. There is no realization without time.

"Good time" is a prison phrase that refers to the ability to do a sentence with a minimum of internal suffering and external trouble with prison authorities. "Hard time" means the opposite: the endurance of time that is filled with trouble, suffering, and ugly entanglements with fellow inmates and with the power structure. The psychological strategy most often recommended by inmates for the accomplishment of good time is to keep a low profile— both with the prison administration and with other inmates. Not to be noticed may be equated with not getting into trouble. This strategy can be difficult for inmates who have short tempers, irritable nervous systems, or just gregarious natures that crave involvement with other people. Younger prisoners especially get into trouble when they act out of distorted egos that are filled with anger, suspicions, and jealousies, and this trouble means hard time. Although older inmates may still have ego distortions, they can also be the source of much stability in a prison community, as they don't have the same needs to prove or defend themselves as do younger inmates. They are often able to calm the overheated tempers of younger prisoners who have difficulty controlling themselves. New inmates are often advised with the old prison adage, "Do your time; don't let the time do you."

Practice can help with the doing of time and keeping a low profile. Sitting-still practice helps to soften or make permeable the ego walls that we often feel defend us from the attacks of others. Meditation does this by demonstrating to us how illusory our ego boundaries can be. Especially when sitting with a group, we begin to notice how our practice can blend into, and be encouraged by, the practice of those around us. Try the next meditation exercise, which is a more advanced concentration on the space between each breath. Let the dimension of time get narrowed to the fraction of a second that lies between each breath.

MEDITATION FIFTEEN: THE SPACE BETWEEN THE BREATH

Settle in your position and take a moment just to be aware of your body and the space (physical, mental, and emotional) in which you find yourself. You can keep your eyes open, with your eyes cast down slightly or, if you prefer, close them. Give your body, and the space inside and out of it, permission to be just as they are in this moment. Just check out the situation of your personal space. Notice the sensations of temperature or pain, tightness or relaxation.

After a minute or so, having checked you body and your surroundings in this way, just let it all be and shift your attention to your breathing. Be aware of the point just below your nostrils where you can feel the air moving in and out. Think of a door swinging gently back and forth. Notice the quality and speed of your breathing without trying to change it. Next, place your attention on the out-breath in particular. With each exhalation, let your attention and sense of being just ride the breath as it flows out and dissolves into the space in front of you. At the end of the exhale, there is a gap before the direction is reversed. Just let yourself rest in that space before the next inhalation; just rest and notice without judgment whatever arises in that space— thoughts, bodily sensations, pain, whatever. Just let your attention hover over that gap between the movement of air out and its next movement in. With the next breath you again follow the exhalation into the space in front of you. Just let your attention go out with the breath and dissolve, resting in the gap before the next inhalation. Continue with the cycle of breathing, concentrating on dissolving with the out-breath and resting in the space before the next in-breath. Let everything else be. Let thoughts or sounds or bodily feelings come and go as they will.

If you get distracted, just notice the sensation, thought, or emotion that took your attention from the breathing cycle. No judgment. Just notice and name what has distracted you: "fear," "tight muscles," "what I have to do tomorrow,": or "pain on the left side of my torso." Then return to your breathing cycle after this noticing has been done. Continue this for as long as you can.

In addition to demonstrating our different experiences of time, meditation can help us to blend in with a group, first with those we meditate with, then with the larger prison community. Sitting practice helps us to observe our fleeting and changing thoughts and emotions. After awhile we start to experience less attachment to our own ideas, and in this way we start to realize that we don't always need to stand out or show off the importance of our own ego or our own opinions. We learn to be content, as Suzuki Roshi once explained, with not leaving traces of ourselves everywhere. We learn to watch serenely as our footprints are erased from the beach by the persistent waves. Like looking up into a clear night of stars, sitting still lets us begin to learn (and not be frightened by) the idea that we, as individuals, are not very important in the larger scheme of things. At first this sounds like a negative, deflating experience, but it is really liberation. It helps us to stop pushing our own version of how things should be with other people, or with the world in general; it makes us less attached to our own ideas. In turn, this softening of the ego starts to improve the human relations around us.

Inmate Gunaratna Sarika, from the Ohio State Prison, mentions how meditation began to help one of the inmates in his practice group. "This guy was always arguing with the guards about one thing or another. Often he was in the right, but we started to ask him if it was worth it. In our situation in here, it doesn't matter if you are right, the power difference between inmates and guards means that their side almost always wins these direct confrontations. After some time sitting with our group, he began to have fewer of these confrontations. He began to see his part in these arguments: his desire to be right, his attachment to his own opinions and his being trapped a cycle that his own righteous anger helped to perpetuate." [1]

UN-DOING TIME

Even a few sessions of sitting meditation will serve to demonstrate the unpredictable nature of the experience of time. In one session, it may seem like years before the bell rings to end the period; but sometimes we are surprised when the bell rings, thinking we have just started to practice. Time is part of our experience of the world, and that experience changes as our mind changes. Everyone is familiar with the slowing of time as we remember in minute detail all the circumstances of an accident or other physical trauma—or the speeding up of time as we enjoy ourselves, lost in some good book or movie.

So time is the prime dimension in prison life as well as in the practice of meditation. Advancing in the practice means being able to experience the present moment in all its brightness and clarity. To do this, we can spend many sessions on the cushion just noticing how many of our thoughts refer to the past, how many are conjectures about the future— and how little of our attention relates to the experience of the present moment. Noticing, checking these out-of-sync thoughts, and returning to the present moment is a simple way of describing what we do inside our heads as we meditate. Dôgen felt that whenever we meditate we are encircled by the three dimensions of time (past, present, and future), but that our sitting can reach to past and future only through the gateway of the deep experience of the present moment. Dôgen also believed that sitting still is, in itself, already enlightenment. This is encouraging.

"Understanding does not await its own arrival" is what Dôgen said about this relationship of practice to time. There is no need, he is telling us, to become preoccupied with the pursuit of some enlightened state that we think only lies somewhere in the future. It is a very comforting thought to remind ourselves that we are already buddhas—long before we thought we were. This intense and consistent attention to the present moment is what makes mindfulness possible and what can gradually change the heavy, ominous, and boring experience of doing time inside. If, after some experience of meditation, we learn how to play a card game or darn a sock with full attention to the activity in the present moment, then this is evidence that mindfulness is beginning to permeate our experience of time.

Indiana State Prison inmate Kerry Greenwell sees time as an opportunity for prisoners. "We have the opportunity to devote all of our time to study and practice, which in turn would not only benefit us, but ultimately all of society, because if the practice is fruitful in here, we could not help but become better human beings. The majority of us [in Indiana State Prison, a maximum security institution] have many years left to our sentences that could be spent cultivating our practice on a much higher level. Through the understanding generated by practice, I find the experience of time to be more simplistic, not near as chaotic and very fulfilling." [2]

THE YOGA OF THE NIGHT

To handle the issue of time—the one abundant commodity in prison life—inmates adopt various strategies. If television is available, it can become a constant consumer of our time. Lost in this electronic bardo state, many prisoners pass day after week after year staring at the flickering screen. (*Bardo* is a Tibetan name for an after-death, in-between state similar to the Catholic concept of purgatory.) Inmates often find that cigarette, drug, and alcohol use are other ways to endure and consume time. Card games and gambling of various sorts take up the time of other inmates. Those prisoners who tend to be gregarious spend most of their time servicing the gossip mill and caught up in the internal politics of the institution.

The other time-eater is sleep. Despite the noise levels in some prisons, many inmates adapt and train themselves to sleep for extended periods, both day and night. Especially in prisons that have few programs, activities, or work opportunities, this strategy is very common. Some prisoners sleep up to ten, twelve, or even sixteen hours a day. Not coincidentally, this lengthening of sleep time is also one of the most common symptoms of clinical depression.

Many Buddhist inmates do sitting meditation sessions late at night or in the early morning to avoid the daytime noise and the self-consciousness of trying to sit still while others are around to watch and comment. I have often noticed that prisoners who have learned breath counting use it to help themselves go to sleep. This did not seem, at first, a good application of this skill, but after several inmates put breath counting to use in this way, I began to agree with them that it is a useful psychological tool. But using breath counting to fall asleep is much different from using it as a focus of concentration during sitting meditation. Meditation should strive to achieve a balance between alertness and relaxation. I think it is better that people not use the same method to fall asleep that they use in meditation. For instance, if they do breath counting to fall asleep, then koan, visualization, or some other form of breath practice should be used during meditation sessions. This avoids the suggestion of drowsiness during meditation that might be produced from the mental association with the same practice used prior to falling asleep.

Time spent sleeping and dreaming can also be used in meditation practice. In a dialogue between His Holiness the Dalai Lama and western scientists, His Holiness talks about one of the many Buddhist strategies for sleep as practice. "In addition to practicing during the waking state, if you can also use your consciousness during sleep for wholesome purposes, then the power of your spiritual practice will be all the greater. Otherwise at least a few hours each night will be just a waste. So if you can transform your sleep into something virtuous, this is useful. The Sutrayana method is to try as you go to sleep to develop a wholesome mental state, such as compassion, or the realization of impermanence or emptiness." [3]

One of the first Buddhist strategies for the yoga of the night is to prepare mentally for sleep with an intentionally cultivated open and positive attitude. Focusing on your own best intentions, you might compose a gatha to say each time you prepare for sleep—something like, "As I prepare my mind and body for sleep, I intend that my dreams be peaceful and clear, that my body gain rest, and that I may awaken rededicated to peace and compassion." It would be good practice to experiment with a sleep gatha that fits your own needs precisely.

The other baseline effort that can turn sleeping and dreaming into practice is to note carefully the processes themselves. Just as in sitting-still meditation we pay attention to the way the mind works—with all the ups and downs that this attention entails—so, too, mindfulness is the connecting link for practicing while in each of the different states of consciousness, including sleep.

Sleep yoga should also include awareness of the processes of falling asleep and of waking. In western culture, we encourage a dualistic attitude: we are either awake or asleep. But, in reality, sleep and waking are not either/or, on/off experiences. For instance, instead of rushing to drink coffee, smoke a cigarette, or consume some other substance that will make us fully awake, we can wake up slowly and become aware of a gradual, intermediate state of consciousness. In the same way, the interested practitioner can learn a lot about his or her consciousness by being mindful (nonjudging and aware) of the process of falling asleep. A gatha might also be used on waking to reset positive intentions for the day ahead—for instance, "Waking up, I give thanks for the opportunity of a new day. I commit myself to the full experience of each moment and I rededicate myself to compassion for all the beings I will meet this day."

Neither western science nor the various streams of Buddhist thought agree on the significance of dreams. Some neuroscientists believe dreams are merely random and meaningless firings of brain circuits—made up of a mixture of the day's events, memories, and sensory images of various sorts. Other, more therapeutically oriented psychologists believe that dreams provide important access to unconscious material. But despite these controversies, we do know that dreaming is necessary for good physical and mental health. We also know that people can train themselves to recall their dreams and can also learn the skill of lucid dreaming. In lucid dreaming, we become aware that we are dreaming—while we are in the dream state. The dreamer can learn to take over the plot and outcome of the dream narrative. This practice may help us to experience a more thorough mastery of our own minds and can train us not to feel like passive victims of our own psychic processes. Like meditation, lucid dreaming is another form of mental training that can subtly change our mental environment over the course of time. A number of books are available about lucid dreaming that the interested practitioner may consult.

It is in prisons, hospitals, and monasteries—sadly or fortunately— that these intermediate daily fluctuations of consciousness may be studied most easily. The lack of the busyness and rushed activity that typifies life in the outside world can help the person inside experience conscious-ness more fully. The stable exterior structure of schedules and familiar physical surroundings facilitates the observation of interior states for those inside. Awareness of these states may be "dharma gates"—explorations of consciousness and possibilities for practice. Handled in this way, the flow of time turns into a resource to be used rather than a condition to be endured.

FINDING A TEACHER

The practitioner in prison can make progress through reading, medita-tion instruction, and participation with an inside sangha. But there comes a time when practice cannot advance without the help of a fully autho-rized teacher. Sometimes, a teacher may already be visiting the prison. In these cases, it is important for the Buddhist inmate to seek out time with this teacher, or if that isn't possible, to set up a letter writing or telephone consultation schedule.

Usually those who volunteer to work inside are authorized to give basic meditation instruction but may not be fully independent teachers who can take on the task of long-term spiritual direction for students. Fellow members of a prison sangha can help with basic "how-to" guid-ance for newcomers, as well as emotional support and encouragement, but they should not be looked to as teachers. In the United States, there are already many instances of teachers who have formed intense, long-term teaching relationships with inmates.

If a teacher is not readily available for personal visitation, you can begin asking around, writing for information, and attempting to make contact with a teacher who fits your personality and practice goals. See who answers your letters, then evaluate the advice they give. Is it realistic for your situation? Sometimes the type of Buddhism available to a par-ticular institution is not the one you care to study with. You might want, for instance, to study in the Tibetan tradition, but only a Pure Land group is visiting the prison. So sometimes it will be necessary to make special efforts to contact an appropriate teacher. At other times, Buddhism may not even be the appropriate arena for an inmate's study, and spiritual direction will come from another faith tradition.

No matter the religion or sect, a teacher or spiritual director should be someone to whom you will listen—even when he or she says difficult or puzzling things—and someone with whom you are willing to enter into a long-term student-teacher relationship. The teacher should be someone whose behavior matches his or her words and whose presence or "vibes" somehow fit with those of the student. Finding the right teacher can be a lifelong process and should be undertaken with great seriousness. Please take as much time as is needed to make this longer-term commitment decision. In addition, people may discover they need different teachers at different times in their lives.

Most fully authorized teachers are very busy people. They often have more people clamoring for their attention than they can possibly take care of. Adding prison visitation or correspondence time to their schedules may be a great sacrifice. Taking on a new student is a big commitment of time and energy. On the other hand, many students in outside sanghas are overly dependent on their teachers—rushing at every opportunity for one-on-one interviews, perhaps rarely showing up for meditation periods unless they know the teacher is going to be there. Few of them may sit daily, but they seem to need validation from outside of themselves, or from another person who they think will give them something they don't already have.

But meditation is empirical. Buddhism is a do-it-yourself practice. Teachers are there to encourage and to confirm progress, to serve as compasses in our spiritual navigation. To extend this metaphor to the student-teacher relationship, many American Buddhists may too often mistake the map for the territory. So perhaps inmates have an advantage in being forced to rely on their own right intentions and their own daily practice while undertaking the search for a teacher. This seeming difficulty may actually help the inmate practitioner to avoid years of thinking the answers are going to come from some guru.

Robert Aitken Roshi, who has worked with prisoners since the late

1950s, emphasizes that prison time might best be spent doing the research, reading, and experiments in practice that will narrow down an inmate's proper niche in the spiritual world. "It's been said that there is a person for every religion and a religion for every person. Every teacher eventually learns that some students are in the wrong place and need to move from Zen to vipassana, for instance, or they should incorporate meditation practice into their own tradition of origin, like Christianity, Islam, or Judaism. So inmates should read extensively and write letters to different groups. See who answers. At least prison gives you the time to find out where you belong."[4] Remember that Buddhism is a trial-and-error, find-out-for-yourself activity. If a teaching relationship doesn't work out, then move on and seek some other arrangement.

SANGHA BUILDING INSIDE

Another activity that can be considered an advanced form of practice is sangha building, which simply means "doing things together." This may sound mundane, but it is an advanced practice. No matter how balanced and peaceful we are when sitting still, the true fruits of practice are shown when we deal with other people. This is where compassion is proven, where mindfulness is tested, and where the precepts flourish or fail.

It only takes three Buddhists to make a sangha—two could call themselves spiritual friends, maybe, but are not quite yet a group. And doing something together might be as simple as establishing a group sitting time once a week in the institution. Yet this seemingly easy activity might take a small inside group anywhere from a month to a year to arrange.

When this is done, the group might try to acquire zafus or other Buddhist materials for group sittings or books for a Buddhist library; or the group might initiate contact with a nearby dharma center. After much careful work with the administration and chaplaincy structure, an ideal inside sangha might manage to gain the use of the chapel or another quiet space for a few hours at least twice a week, with enough time for at least two sitting meditation sessions, walking meditation in between, and some brief socializing time afterward. In addition to this weekly activity, a once-a-month dharma talk from an outside sangha teacher would be important to inside practice. If no one from an outside group is able to come, then in place of a dharma talk there could be a group reading of a Buddhist book, followed by a discussion. Discussion leadership should be rotated among the sangha members regardless of seniority.

As mentioned in previous chapters, prison sanghas need to be very careful about issues of power and status: How does the group make decisions and how do activities get done? To avoid power-tripping by more dominant members, I would suggest not even appointing or electing any kind of officers for the first year or so—or until this seems absolutely necessary. No fundraising should be undertaken until some clear need for it is agreed on by the group. A different facilitator may be chosen to lead each sangha meeting. Coordinators for sangha activities could be volunteers serving on an ad hoc basis for only one event at a time. Such an arrangement gives everyone an opportunity to give to the group and also diffuses the power issues. All decisions should be made by the procedures of consensus.

Inside sanghas often function well when they are focused on obtaining the permissions and resources needed to practice. Opposition from chaplains or administrators helps to strengthen the resolve and commitment of inside Buddhists. But after these things have been achieved, the sangha sometimes has trouble between members. A common enemy creates unity; when the apparent enemy goes away, we are left to fight among ourselves. Peacemaking and efforts toward harmony with each other and with other inside groups should be the primary goal of sangha building. When a common "enemy" disappears, it is sometimes very helpful to replace the focus with a common service goal for the sangha. Working toward prison rape prevention or interracial reconciliation or attempting to create better understanding between Muslim and Buddhist or Christian and Buddhist groups inside are examples of possible service activities. Volunteering with sick or dying inmates, getting a garden or adult education project going, soliciting book donations for a spiritual practices library, writing letters for others, and tutoring inmates who can't read—all these are possibilities for advancing the Buddhist practice of compassion in the real world of prison life.

Another activity that may be carried out without outside help could be a monthly meeting in which the group recites the precepts together. Before or after the recitation, individuals may talk about what difficulties they have had with the precepts in the last month and identify goals for improving their faithfulness to these traditional guidelines. This regular practice is very powerful and practical and has a long traditional history in monastic Buddhism. Precept recitation is an important part of sangha building that allows for corrections of attitudes and behaviors and helps to mend rifts in the community. It also keeps reminding us of our highest intentions.

Once a weekly and monthly schedule is operating successfully, the group might want to celebrate one or two Buddhist holidays each year— Buddha's birthday and enlightenment are the two most common in mahayana traditions. Dates and descriptions of these and other holidays are given in John Snelling's *A Buddhist Handbook*. Buddhists in Northern California (where there are communities of Buddhists from almost every conceivable lineage and ethnicity) have been celebrating "Buddha Day" together for almost two decades. Based on a Theravada Festival, this event is designed to bring together all Buddhists in a joint celebration of the historical Buddha's birth and enlightenment. Buddha Day is a good possibility for prisons, whose rules often allow only one religious holiday yearly for each inmate religion. This combined holiday is also a good idea for those lucky places that have more than one sect of Buddhism active among inmates.

Many Buddhist traditions use two easy-to-remember dates as major holidays: April 8 for Buddha's birthday and December 8 for Buddha's enlightenment day. A good number of prison dharma groups have now been able to celebrate these holidays with special ceremonies, meals, and visitors from the outside. Calvin Malone, an inmate at Washington's Airway Heights Correction Center, writes that Buddhist inmates there put together an annual "Freedom Celebration," starting in May 1996. They faced many institutional obstacles and outright sabotages, but with perseverance and patience the event finally happened. The celebration includes the participation of about forty inmates and up to thirty outside visitors and family members. In 1997, Malone wrote about that first event. "Last year we held our first annual event, FREEDOM CELEBRATION 96. Thirty-six inmates attended as well as nineteen guests from Oregon, Montana, and all around Washington. This celebration turned out to be a huge success and is still discussed around this prison. There was a program of short talks, music, a play, and a banquet. This event left a positive impression on everyone. During the event the AHCC Superintendent, Kay Walter, stated that our event was the best organized, most focused event she had attended in her capacity as superintendent, she said it had a good feel." [5]

Working together to create such celebrations serves to increase the bonds between sangha members as well as the sangha's legitimacy with the authorities. Sangha members involved in the planning get a chance to practice patience and compassion as they handle the many obstacles that seem to especially upset first-time celebrations. An unexpected lockdown, for instance, forced the Indiana State Prison sangha to reschedule a celebration. "Lost" paperwork, with requests for special visitors or other needed arrangements, created difficulties for several sanghas. Organizational obstacles also come from inmates themselves. At one prison, an inmate (who requests anonymity) writes:

> The feast situation is becoming sort of bizarre. Historically, the Visakha Puja includes a vegetarian feast, but most of our members want to order such things as sweet and sour chicken or chicken chow mein. What makes this interesting is that some of our members are actually Muslims who came to learn to meditate and they are the ones mostly in favor of these chicken-based goods. I'm at a loss as to how to get everyone to understand why we shouldn't include meat in the feast. Prob-

ably we will split the order and end up with meat and
vegetarian food. I find this all very amusing. [6]

A certain amount of spiritual materialism may often be involved in
Buddhist prison celebrations; in this example, prison rules allowing special meals for religious holidays made participation attractive to many
inmates who desperately craved a chance for variety in food. Having
visitors attend from the outside is also an attraction, as is the prospect of
donations and other demonstrations of support that may be generated
by such celebrations. But these planning and preparation periods can
also be a way to educate others about Buddhist beliefs and customs and
to give inmates opportunities to feel the joys and challenges involved in
bringing off any successful religious celebration, whether a Christmas
pageant or a Buddha's birthday ceremony. The important thing is to let
the challenges strengthen the group rather than create divisions. In these
ways, such holiday preparations can become real community-building
and sangha-validating activities.

RETREATS INSIDE

Another group goal could be to negotiate a full daylong retreat for the
inside sangha several times per year. Called zazenkai in some Japanese
traditions, or sesshin, or a day of mindfulness, this kind of mini-retreat
gives inside practitioners the important experience of more intensive practice. Some institutions have even allowed three-, five-, or seven-day retreats to take place, but the likelihood of obtaining such permissions is
sometimes slim because of the logistical barriers. One-day sittings are a
good place to start, because they are easier to organize and accomplish.
Getting through a full day of meditation for the first time is also a great
boost and encouragement to the new meditator. In a one-day or more
extended retreat, inmates can experience the shortening and lengthening
of time and a deep and powerful meditative experience that comes when
effort is sustained and the mind can settle itself deeply—hard to duplicate either sitting alone or sitting in a group for just one or two periods.

In one Buddhist tradition, that of the Indian vipassana teacher S. N. Goenka, the ten-day retreat format is the only form that is practiced. Prison administrations worldwide have been challenged to allow for this religious requirement, but with administrative cooperation such a retreat can be accomplished. A ten-day vipassana retreat was once held for one thousand inmates in India's notorious Tihan Prison outside New Delhi. In 1997, teachers in Goenka's lineage conducted the first ten-day U.S. prison retreat at Seattle's North Rehabilitation Facility, which houses about forty female and two hundred and fifty male inmates. A great deal of flexibility and cooperation was required of the administration and staff to host one of these ten-day retreats. The inmate participants had to be together twenty-four hours a day, and so special rooms had to be allocated. Volunteers from the security and counseling staffs attended the retreat along with the inmates, which simplified the security issue. Head counts are conducted in all prisons at fixed hours, depending on the institution, every day of the year. These security procedures are meant to detect missing inmates and need to be done even during a one-day retreat. The watch commanders at Seattle agreed to let the volunteer staff phone in the head counts at times convenient to the retreat schedule. Special arrangements also had to be made for the delivery of vegetarian meals during the days of the retreat. From an administrative point of view, these retreats may be seen as nothing but logistical nightmares, for good reason.

Even in the ten-day format of S. N. Goenka, the first three days are a time of settling, and breath meditation is the primary technique. Three days also seems to be the norm for getting through the leg and back pain that is such a challenge for any longer retreat. As the mind settles, retreat participants begin to experience physiological and mental phenomena that are rarely noticed in normal consciousness. Sleep and dream states can intrude into the sitting periods. Distracting and unusual bodily sensations often occur. States of panic, elation, or anger might sweep away all concentration and tranquility. The meditator begins to realize the impermanence of all these states and to experience an almost warriorlike satisfaction in his or her ability to sit through all of these mental and physical phenomena. Inmates who have successfully completed longer prison retreats have noticed great changes in their thinking about themselves and in their behavior toward others.

These changes are also obvious to staff and other inmates. Laine Moore, a security guard in the women's unit of North Rehabilitation Facility, taught an informal introductory meditation class for the women one night per week—on her own time. When permission was granted for the men to do a ten-day vipassana retreat, she was able to observe the results of this more intensive practice.

> I thought the male retreat was so interesting, so I went and did the ten-day Vipassana program on the outside so that I could help if we did another retreat for the women. I wanted to be involved because with the classes I was doing, I knew the women only got a glimpse of the effects of meditation. But after the ten-day session with the women inmates, I noticed a real difference in the dormitory; it was more peaceful, they got along better. I had always kept my own meditation practice private because I always had a fear of religion in prisons. I was afraid they would think I was trying to force some religion on them. I've found that people are hungry for it in here. At the same time, though, the residents sometimes have a fear of betraying their own religion. [7]

There is certainly no doubt about the benefits of extended practice retreats. What was so unusual in the Seattle situation was the cooperation of the administration and some of the counseling and security staff, whose ability to work together overcame the many institutional obstacles that often arise. The ten-day format of Goenka's vipassana tradition can only work when the highest authority in the institution is willing to support it. It is noteworthy that in both India and Seattle the institutional obstacles were overcome through the efforts of women prison administrators, who were also willing to do the ten-day retreats themselves, before bringing the practice to their institutions.

AWAKENING THE GUARDS

Seattle's Laine Moore is the only prison guard I have found in the course of research for this book who practices meditation and who is helping to advocate for it as a regular part of programs available to inmates, but there certainly must be others. Her unique viewpoint leads us to a discussion of meditation for security personnel.

Robert Aitken Roshi points out that in many U.S. cities, family dynasties of policemen and firemen go back for generations. These public safety jobs are virtually passed down from father to son to grandson, and such families take great pride in this tradition and in their work for the public good. But it is rare to see a second-generation prison guard. Speaking of some of her colleagues, Laine Moore says that "maybe ninety something percent of them have very negative attitudes, and some see their job as just a place to come to catch up on their reading." There is no status in being a prison guard, which can be miserable, boring, and, occasionally, frightening work. But Moore comments on how meditation has helped her change the negative experience of her workplace.

> The basic principle of cause and effect is one thing that guards could learn from meditation and compassion practice. The staff I work with are not taking care of themselves nutrition and healthwise, and they can get very negative. We all know it's not working. The government won't solve this. Both staff and inmates who care must decide that something has to be done and get to work doing it. We need treatment in jails and prisons. Staff often don't want to deal with people, and we get into ego and power struggles. "What I say goes," is an attitude that makes residents feel worthless and then they act as if they have no worth. Guards and inmates

have to discover that cooperation is the best principle.
I always tell the residents that I have a commitment to
enforce the rules, but I will do my best for them if they
cooperate. Meditation is part of my practice of health,
and it makes me feel that my job is wonderful! I can get
along with inmates that no one else can. I have fun.
But it's still hard work. [8]

Security personnel, in their attitudes and behaviors on the job, may
hold the key to their own happiness or misery. It may not be until prison
administrations start to pay close attention to the health and stress issues
of their employees that some of the problems in the prison environment
can be solved. Meditation is certainly not the only answer, but treated as
one part of a more comprehensive employee health and destressing policy,
it could yield powerful results with the underpaid and stigmatized prison
security force. National leaders in the corrections field admit to the
problems in the present situation. Jack Cowley, a thirty-year veteran of
the Oklahoma Department of Corrections, says that "the current system
is not working, and yet more prisons are being constructed and more
people are being incarcerated." He points out that 90 percent of all
inmates will eventually go back to the community, and yet punitive public attitudes seem to drive the politicians who appoint the corrections
administrators. He says that important programs, such as college courses,
have been taken away because of political decisions, even though security personnel and administrators know that such programs reduce disciplinary problems inside and increase the likelihood for inmates to suc-
ceed after release. Cowley hopes that security professionals will begin to
actively educate legislative and community groups rather than enduring
the stereotyping and condescension that has been their social legacy. [9]

Part of the dysfunction of prisons—the "not working" that Cowley
and others have described—has to do with these public attitudes toward
security personnel, who are often portrayed as sadistic, pot-bellied
rednecks with little education and less enthusiasm for their jobs. As with
all stereotypes, a certain amount of truth may exist in these public distor-

tions, but with better training and professional standards, some prison systems are trying to overcome these old images. Security personnel are all too aware of these public attitudes, which add negativity and devaluation to their already stressful working lives.

In India, before being able to stage her one-thousand-man vipassana retreat at Tihan Prison, the warden sent her cruelest, most corrupt, and most troubled security guards to outside vipassana retreats. This action laid the ground for change in the institutional atmosphere, which had to precede the staff cooperation needed to accomplish the inmate retreats. Real change must be reinforced from all sides. The public, the guards, and the inmates must all take responsibility for training their minds and for grounding their behaviors in compassion.

RESTORATION

Not much has been mentioned in this book about the original crimes that brought us to prison. For many inmates, prison time is the worst thing that ever happened to them, and yet the present criminal justice system does not encourage any accurate examination of the behavior that led to incarceration. From a Buddhist point of view, the precipitating crime is a very important karmic (cause and effect) event. We must acknowledge that rarely does criminal behavior come out of nowhere. There is a pattern of thought and action to be examined.

One of the results of extended meditation practice is an increased ability to observe accurately the ongoing procession of thoughts and emotions. This ability to observe can help lead us to a very matter-of-fact honesty about why we are in prison. Sometimes it takes years for this kind of internal honesty to replace the memorized and rehearsed stories we tell ourselves and others, about why we are in prison. These almost automatic stories are a result of our own denial and minimizing, as well as the distortion caused by long legal defense battles that overtly or covertly encourage silence about the criminal act. In the U.S. legal system, innocence must be declared in order to get the full benefits of American justice. Few attorneys counsel their clients to admit and ac-

cept guilt for their crimes, at least until sentencing for a guilty verdict—
at which point it is beneficial to demonstrate remorse.

These skewed stories about our crimes are often encouraged by the
language and belief system of social science, which emphasizes childhood trauma and other psychological factors mitigating guilt. Inmates
learn to use this form of rhetoric for the benefit of the courts, penal
psychologists, chaplains, and parole boards. Memorized phrases like "poor
self-esteem" quickly become part of the internal defense against looking
honestly at past misdeeds. Howard Zehr, a professor of sociology and an
expert in "restorative justice," talks about this weakness in our present
criminal justice system.

> Little in the justice process encourages offenders to un-
> derstand the consequences of their actions or to empa-
> thize with victims. On the contrary, the adversarial game
> requires offenders to look out for themselves. Offend-
> ers are discouraged from acknowledging their responsi-
> bility and are given little opportunity to act on this re-
> sponsibility in concrete ways. . . . The stereotypes and
> rationalizations that offenders use to distance themselves
> from the people they hurt are never challenged. So the
> sense of alienation from society experienced by many
> offenders, the feeling that they themselves are victims,
> is only heightened by the legal process and the prison
> experience. [10]

Sitting-still practice can help us see, from a Buddhist perspective,
the underlying human weakness that was involved in our crimes. The
traditional trinity of greed, hatred, and ignorance is an easy framework
from which to start an accurate reconstruction of our internal crime
story—a revised story without the evasions, omissions, and excuses that
have surrounded our previous, automatic and self-excusing story entitled,
"Why I Am in Prison."

I'm not denying that many inmates have suffered brain trauma, childhood abuse, and inherited propensities toward addiction or severe mental illnesses—all of which contribute to the chain of cause and effect that led to incarceration. But, in these cases, part of the inmate's obligation is to undertake a frank recognition of these conditions and adopt a willingness to seek the appropriate treatment, medication, or twelve-step support that can help his or her condition. Buddhist meditation is not the treatment of choice for alcoholism, attention deficit disorder, depression, or schizophrenia. Inmates have an obligation for self-restoration, which means undertaking remedies in addition to whatever spiritual support comes from sitting-still practice.

The concept of restorative justice is one of the few new ideas in American criminology—a field that has seemed empty of new ideas about social reform or personal change. Even in an era when adult violent crime has been decreasing steadily for years, public opinion is inflamed by the media, which loves to focus on sensational crimes. Ratings-boosting stories increase public fears and create an attitude of exasperation. The public begins to say, in effect: Build more prisons, lock up more people, AND throw away the keys. The former corrections ideology of rehabilitation has, unfortunately, also been thrown away with the keys, and the push to have rehabilitation programs inside prisons has almost totally vanished. Basic approaches—such as adult education, physical exercise, counseling, and medical care—are almost nonexistent in many facilities. Remedy comes only occasionally in the form of court-ordered takeovers of facilities that have been overcrowded for year after year, with no relief. The settlement of an American Civil Liberties Union lawsuit, for instance, was the only intervention that was able to budge the Hawaii Department of Public Safety to reduce its overcrowded facilities.

The popular idea that prisoners are set into some rigid criminal personality and do not want to change is not borne out by experience. Most inmates do want to change—the problem is learning how. Lucia Meijer, the Seattle prison administrator who brought vipassana meditation into her facility, talks about the male and female inmates who volunteered to participate in the ten-day retreats:

Our residents have very low frustration thresholds. They

have trouble sitting still or paying attention. And some of them are very heavy smokers. The thing that impressed me more than anything was that they were voluntarily giving up the comforts that are prized in jail—things like phone calls, reading, cigarettes, letters. And they were doing all this in the hope that they might be able to change. There is no reward or advantage for doing these retreats: no reduction in time, no letters to take to the judge. To me, this is evidence that they really do want to change. [11]

The concepts embodied in restorative justice began in the juvenile justice systems of Canada and the United States as commonsense interventions by probation officers with their youthful clients. These interventions often meant taking the offenders to the homes of their victims and encouraging apology, restitution, and reconciliation of all parties. Howard Zehr says that "restorative justice begins with a concern for victims and how to meet their needs, for repairing the harm as much as possible, both concretely and symbolically." [12] Principles learned from community policing, conflict arbitration, and the victims' rights movement, have also helped seed the restorative justice trend, which has the potential to revolutionize how we deal with crime. In the best forms of its implementation, restorative justice can be a healing strategy for both perpetrator and victim; it emphasizes individual responsibility and admission of guilt and goes counter to the silence and evasion encouraged by the procedures of our court systems.

For the inmate practitioner, restorative justice may be seen to follow a long Buddhist tradition of peacemaking, repentance, and responsibility for harm caused. Advancing in practice inside means, first of all, not distorting the thinking that surrounds the crime and the punishment. Mindful restorative action should then follow as a form of personal and social restitution. Such action may take many forms, depending on the history of the crime and the inmate's current situation. The inmate might write to victims or victims' families to acknowledge and apologize for the crime. It is true that such apologies are sometimes rejected, but the attempt has value, even if it only expresses the inmate's hope for changed behavior in the future. In some cases that involve money and property, restitution may be as clear-cut as setting up a plan to repay what was stolen or destroyed. Restoration may also involve overtures to an inmate's own family, who may have been alienated by shame or distance. These efforts sometimes mean writing over and over again with no expectation of reply. Sometimes, though, the inmate's efforts can result in lasting reconciliation. The point is to make the attempt. The point is to experience the simple Buddhist truth that every action has consequences, every action is just one link in a long karmic chain of cause and effect.

The "purification" chant, recited in Zen and other Buddhist services, could be used by inmates as a frequent gatha. The verse may be thought of as the repetition of a vow. Recitation of this verse, mentally or out loud, helps move the mind in the direction of acknowledging and repairing past evils.

> *All the evil karma, ever created by me since of old;*
> *on account of my beginningless greed, hatred and ignorance;*
> *born of my conduct, speech and thought;*
> *I now confess openly and fully.* [13]

FROM INSIDE TO OUT

For inmates who are approaching release, the transition from prison to life outside is a critical time. But formal government assistance with the transition process is harder and harder to come by in the present atmosphere of budget tightening and throw-away-the-key penal philosophy. Even "gate money," which was usually provided to help prisoners set up life outside and span the gap to legitimate livelihood, is very scarce these days.

The issue of assistance with release is a real challenge for outside sanghas. As inmates who have practiced over a period of time come out, the role of the sangha in helping with that process needs to be defined.

One Buddhist teacher commented that the prison system he works with has a rule that religious volunteers cannot have any contact with inmates after they are released. If they do, the sangha's privilege of inside visitation will be taken away. This nonsensical and arbitrary rule gave rise to the following situation. When an inmate sangha member was released, the institution gave him forty dollars in gate money, not even enough for one night's food and lodging. When the just-released inmate called for help, the sangha had to arrange for another Buddhist in a different town to come to his aid—someone he did not know and with whom he had no established relationship.

The inadequacy or lack of release assistance from the penal systems creates important questions for the sanghas who work in prisons. How involved do we want to become in the release process? Can we provide shelter in sangha centers to released inmates? Will providing help make sangha members nervous or fearful? Sometimes it is hard enough just to keep up a commitment to visit an institution on a regular basis; getting involved in work that requires even more commitment and risk may be beyond the capability of many sanghas. Yet assistance with the release transition is one of the most pressing needs for inmates. Bo Lozoff, with decades of experience in prison work behind him, sees this issue as crucial for inmates, and for society at large.

> Right now the biggest need in all of prison work is for postrelease support. The prisons take a guy who's been inside for, say, seventeen years, and they give him a short-sleeve shirt and fifty dollars and out he goes. And then we wonder why he doesn't make it! Most don't have any family or friends left to help. It's almost impossible to predict from behavior inside what will happen after release. Some will continue spiritual practice and others won't.
>
> Being released is stepping out into an abyss. We have to remember that there is this huge sensory buffet waiting to be explored when someone leaves—and many

want to make up for lost time. We run one postrelease
place: Kindness House. But we need many more Kindness Houses. Sanghas and other religious groups should
be providing places where these guys can get help with
finding work and with general trouble-shooting in the
real world. [14]

Most inmates who have gone to live at Buddhist centers after release
have not stayed long. It may be that they feel they have gone from one
prison to another. Geoffrey Shugen Arnold, coordinator of Zen Mountain Monastery's National Prison Project, says that his monastery has
hosted several postrelease inmates, but none have remained. Parole of an
inmate directly to a sangha also has legal dimensions that may scare away
some dharma groups. It may be better for groups who want to help with
postrelease needs to form strong alliances with local social services and
other religious groups in the community. The inmate would participate
in meditation practice like any layperson—at his or her own discretion;
the sangha could provide mentoring, advocacy, and other appropriate
services as needed.

Inmates who are sex offenders present a very strong challenge to the
compassion of outside sanghas. When released, these former inmates are
often subject to registration and notification statutes, which could mean
that neighbors of a sangha would be notified if such an individual took
up residence at a dharma center. Our society has so heavily stigmatized
sex offenders that the label will remain with a person for life. A few social
scientists have appeared in the media, saying, in effect, that sex offenders
cannot be reformed. Although the evidence is quite to the contrary, this
information has not deterred hysteria in these cases. One dharma center
backed off from accepting a postrelease sex offender because the group
feared liability and neighborhood relation issues. "We have families here,"
sangha members said in their own defense.

No inmate knows for certain how he or she will do when released.
For instance, prisoners with a history of alcoholism who faithfully attend inside Alcoholics Anonymous meetings and maintain abstinence

within the prison environment still have no way of knowing absolutely if they will drink or not when released. Leaving prison can be a very frightening, delicate, and difficult time for any inmate. Buddhist groups or individuals who hope to help inmates in this transition process must be prepared for both wonderful outcomes and sad reverses.

Male inmates often find it especially hard to ask for help—responding to how our society trains its men. But in planning for release, the inmate needs to be very active in seeking out as much support as possible for reentry. Help from a sangha, church groups, ex-convict support groups, social services, and family should all be sought out. Asking for help can be a practice in egolessness, like bowing, or like letting other people hold their own opinions. The provision of compassionate and patient mentoring, delivered in a low-key style, can get around some of these ego issues.

Both sitting-still practice and twelve-step ideology can help with the transition process. "A day at a time" would be the appropriate AA saying; "a breath at a time" might be the response based on mindfulness practice. Just as time slows down during crucial karmic events, so time during release and adjustment to freedom may have its own slowed-down quality. In fact, slowing down deliberately could be important counsel to those just released. Because of the sense of life missed or foregone, some inmates feel they have to make up for lost time; but slower, in this case, is always better. Keeping up a commitment to daily practice on return to the outside world could be a pivotal element in the success or failure of reentry.

Engaged Buddhist inmates and outside sanghas committed to prison work may want to look closely at transition needs. Perhaps the creation of small, intentional communities of former inmates would help in this process. Aside from the logistics of food, shelter, and work, released inmates need support to redefine themselves. Instead of adopting the ex-con stigma, former inmates and their supporters can work toward a more positive postrelease identity—an identity of pride in the fact of having "paid one's debt" to society, of having survived incarceration, and of having done the difficult character work that results in lasting change. Life on the outside could then be lived without shame and with openness to the wider world of practice, work, and relationships.

REFORMING PRISONS, RE-FORMING PEOPLE

Prison reform itself may be looked upon as a way of engaged Buddhism, as a practice of service and generosity that includes inmates, guards, families, and outside volunteers. The inmate who founded the Springfield hospice program is firm in his belief that the initiative for reform must happen from both inside and out. "If prisoners truly want to see prison reform, they must initiate it themselves with the support of their families on the outside. Upon release the ex-offender probably won't do much about prison reform; he has enough to do just trying to put his life back together. So the change has to come from the inside. The trouble is that most inmates feel helpless or scared. They don't think the prison will allow change or reform. This is true. The old system does, in fact, put up one heck of a struggle against any change. But if enough people try, the timing and opportunity eventually presents itself." [16]

Dharma teachers who have worked with prison sanghas seem to agree that the most common issue for inside practitioners is how to get along with difficult fellow inmates. This is probably the most punishing of all the aspects of prison life, as society's most crazy, violent, and dangerous people are locked inside prisons. Dealing with problematic inmate neighbors is one of the things that can make time inside into hard time. An inside sangha may want to spend a good deal of its group time together—in addition to paying attention to mindfulness with other sangha members—helping and encouraging each other to make peace with other inmates and sharing the skillful compassion needed to survive inside without creating more hatred, suspiciousness, and mental anguish.

Sanghas inside must also be careful with the issue of recruitment. We would all do well to remember the importance of "attraction rather than promotion," as the twelve-step programs put it. Sangha building is not a numbers game or a competition with other religions. It isn't anyone's job to convince people that their faith tradition, or their lack of one, is wrong. Three earnest sitters can be a fully functioning sangha. Start there.

Outside volunteers may also help through political education and community advocacy. Most prison administrators know that the present situation is not working, yet they feel at the mercy of public attitudes and the policymaking knee-jerks of legislators worried about being thought soft on crime. Outside people can do a lot to assist in the changing of public attitudes and in the education of politicians. And as Laine Moore points out, security personnel can be very helpful in this effort to educate and change. There are some hopeful signs for the future. Buddhist groups like the Prison Dharma Network, Buddhist Peace Fellowship, and Zen Mountain Monastery have begun to increase their national profiles in the coordination of services for inmates. *Turning Wheel*, the journal published by the BPF, is now dedicating a full page of every issue to prison dharma. The *Shambhala Sun*, a national Buddhist magazine, also runs frequent features by Bo Lozoff, Fleet Maull, and others who have been active in contemplative prison practice. Word is getting out; the public is becoming more educated, and this fact will help inmates and their guards to feel that they have not been abandoned.

There are some basic economic and political structural changes that all of us need to worry about and monitor. As the movement toward privatization of prisons proceeds, the housing of inmates has become a big, free-market business. Real estate investment trusts (REITs), specializing in prison properties, are now sold on the stock market. Corrections Corporation of America, with assets in the billions of dollars, has been buying up smaller prison companies and is fast becoming an unregulated monopoly in the U.S. economy. To keep their properties filled, such large companies hope for longer sentences and provide fewer rehabilitation services inside, as these services can be costly and weaken the corporate bottom line. Successful rehabilitation also lowers recidivism, which further damages long-term corporate profits. Like hotels, prison companies must concern themselves with the economics of occupancy rates.

Defense companies have also retooled, after post-cold-war U.S. military spending cuts. They now find a ready market for weapons and high-tech security paraphernalia among the nation's police departments and prisons. Smalltown sheriffs now boast of helicopters and armored personnel carriers provided to them by the Pentagon. Prison administrators delight in showing off the new equipment used by specially trained tactical squads in their maximum-security "control units." Inmates are increasingly being denied visitation and free-speech rights at the whims of state politicians or institutional administrators. All these changes converge to make the prison of the future a playland of macho toys and secure perimeters where the human inhabitants, both inmates and guards, are devalued and oppressed. All of us have an obligation to work against these trends and encourage programs based on restorative justice, good counseling, medical care, and education for prisoners.

REAL TIME

Time is the punishment and time is the reward. If viewed as reward, the hard time of prison can be transformed by Buddhist practice into the real time of awakening with each moment. Like the legendary alchemists who could change lead into gold, inmates can transform the leaden time of prison sentences into the real time of lives lived moment-by-moment, fully conscious and fully awake to the world. Mindfulness practice (living fully in each moment) connects each element of daily experience: sleeping, eating, exercising, and sitting-still meditation.

In Buddhist thinking, time does not go only in one direction. The present is the real time, the point of entry into past or future. The past wraps itself around the present moment—as does the future. If change is to happen, it can only happen in the present moment. Change is now. Anything else is promise or regret. Don't wait for anything to arrive—whether that thing is enlightenment or release from prison or understanding of the Great Matter. Remember Dôgen's words: "Understanding does not await its own arrival." To live anywhere—inside or out—is to do time. Time is the raw material of our waking up.

There is a certain pace and regularity to the passage of time inside. How practice can entwine with this daily regularity is well described in a poem, called "The Buddha Awakens" by prison writer Kent Wimberly, who practices at the Donovan Federal Penitentiary in Southern California. In the poem, he describes the process of mindfulness at work in prison life, from waking, into daytime activity, into formal meditation consciousness. Some days are filled with good time, other days are filled with hard time—but, as an old Zen teacher said, "Every day is a good day." Every day, whether we call it good or bad, gives each of us the opportunity to awaken together in real time.

THE BUDDHA AWAKENS *by Kent Wimberly* [16]

WHAHHHH WHAH-WHAHH WHAHH WHAHH.
Prison guard with a mouth full of marbles.
Early morning wake-up call.
Concrete. Steel. Prison cell. Home.

Thursday, Thursday, Thursday.
Cell mate works this morning. My day-off from exercising.
Work this afternoon. My Friday.
Life is good.

Morning's first light shining through the window.
The sound of distant toilets flushing.
Cellie stirring.
Time to get up.

Quiet, quiet, like a cat
Get dressed. Brush my teeth.
Clink of the toothbrush against the shelf.
Careful. Mindful.

Rumble and hiss of the ventilation duct.
I breathe. The prison breathes.

I'm in the belly of a great beast.
Wash my face. Comb my hair. Make a funny face in the mirror.

Denim clad corpuscles careening through capillaries of the beast.
Receive nourishment. Deliver energy.
Repair damaged structures.
Live. Reproduce. Die.
Thursday, Thursday, Thursday.

. . . Guards at the dining room door.
Dour faces. Watching the animals.
Protruding into our world. But not penetrating.
Well, sometimes.
Chow hall.
Blast of moist heat.
Smells of fried eggs and wet mops.
Noise. Bad manners. Dirty dishes. Ruined food.

. . . Take the long capillary back to my cell . . .
Thursday, Thursday, Thursday.
Cellie is at work when I get home.
Peace, quiet, solitude. A hot cup of coffee.
It's great to be alive!
Folded blankets. One for the floor, two to sit on.
Posture. Breathing. Labeling.
Rumble and hiss of ventilation. Distant toilets. A radio.
I breathe. The beast breathes.

I awaken the Buddha.

CHAPTER 8 NOTES

The epigram is from Eihei Dôgen, "The Time Being, Uji," in *Moon in a Dewdrop*, ed. Kazuaki Tanahashi (San Francisco: North Point Press, 1985), 77.

1. Gunaratna Sarika, personal communication, 1998.

2. Kerry J. Greenwell, personal communication, 1997.

3. His Holiness the Dalai Lama, in *Sleeping, Dreaming, and Dying*, ed. Francisco J. Varela (Boston: Wisdom Publications, 1997), 124.

4. Robert Aitken, personal communication, 1998.

5. Calvin Malone, personal communication, 1997.

6. Anonymous, personal communication, 1997.

7. Laine Moore, personal communication, 1998.

8. Ibid.

9. Jack Cowley, "Changing Public Opinion," *Corrections Today* (American Corrections Association), February 1998, 39.

10. Howard Zehr, "Restorative Justice: The Concept," *Corrections Today*, December 1997, 68.

11. Lucia Meijer, personal communication, 1998.

12. Zehr, "Restorative Justice," 68.

13. "Purification," *Diamond Sangha Sutra Book*, typescript, 1.

14. Bo Lozoff, personal communication, 1998.

15. Anonymous, personal communication, 1997.

16. Kent Wimberly, "The Buddha Awakens," personal communication, typescript, 1997.

BIBLIOGRAPHY

These books are recommended for individual inmates, prison dharma groups or prison libraries. They will help any inmate or staff member who wants to learn the basics of Buddhist history, teachings and meditation techniques. I have included books that discuss the meditation techniques from several Buddhist traditions including Vipassana, Zen, Theravada, and Tibetan.

Robert Aitken, *Taking the Path of Zen*, North Point Press (New York, 1982). An excellent, practical guide to the Zen style of sitting meditation.

Karen Anderson, *Buddha,* Penguin Putnam Group (New York, 2001). A nonsectarian and well written biography of the historical Buddha's life. Anderson, a well-known historian of religion, uses her scholarship to set the Buddha's life within its historical and cultural context.

Stephen Batchelor, *Buddhism Without Beliefs: A Contemporary Guide to Awakening,* Riverhead Books (New York, 1997). A clear retelling of the Buddha's discovery of the four noble truths.

Herbert Bensen, *The Relaxation Response*, Avon Books (New York, 1975). An excellent guide to secular, non-religious meditation.

Pema Chodron, *Start Where You Are.* Shambhala (Boston, 1994).

Pema Chodron, *Wisdom of No Escape.* Shambhala (Boston, 1991).

Thomas Cleary (translator), *Minding Mind: A Course in Basic Meditation*, Shambhala Publications (Boston, 1995). Translations of the meditation manuals written by seven old masters from China, Korea, and Japan.

Roger J. Corless, *The Vision of Buddhism*, Paragon House (New York, 1989). Good overview of the history and teachings of the many sects of Buddhism.

Bernie Glassman, *Bearing Witness*. Bell Tower (1998). Contains chapter detailing Fleet Maull's prison experience and transformation.

Palden Gyatso, *The Autobiography of a Tibetan Monk*, Grove Press (New York, 2000).

Henepola Gunaratana, *Mindfulness in Plain English*, Wisdom Publications (Boston, 1992). An eloquent discussion of mindfulness from a vipassana perspective.

Bo Lozoff, *We're All Doing Time: A Guide for Getting Free*, Human Kindness Foundation (Durham, 1995). Although not technically confined to Buddhism, this book has been available free to prisoners for more than a decade and contains perennial wisdom from many traditions. Introduction by His Holiness the Dalai Lama.

Kathleen McDonald, *How to Meditate*, Wisdom Publications (Boston, 1984). An excellent introduction to Tibetan meditation techniques from the Gelugpa Tradition.

John Powers, *A Concise Encyclopedia of Buddhism,* Oneworld Publications (Oxford, 2000).

Chogyam Trungpa, *Myth of Freedom,* Shambhala Publications (Boston, 1987).

Chogyam Trungpa, *Cutting Through Spiritual Materialism,* Shambhala Publications (Boston, 1987).

Chogyam Trungpa, *Shambhala: The Sacred Path fo the Warrior,* Shambhala Publications (Boston, 1988).

Walpola Rahula, *What the Buddha Taught*, Gordon Fraser (Bedford U.K., 1972).

Sharon Salzberg, *Loving-Kindness: The Revolutionary Art of Happiness,* Shambhala Publications (Boston, 1995).

Shunryu Suzuki, *Zen Mind, Beginner's Mind,* Weatherhill (New York, 1970). Simple and encouraging guide to getting started in meditation.

RECOMMENDED READING
FOR PRISON DHARMA VOLUNTEERS

Daniel Burton-Rose, Ed., *The Celling of America: An Inside Look at the U.S. Prison Industry,* Common Courage Press (Monroe, 1998).

Stephen Donaldson, *Manual/Overview of the Prisoner Rape Project,* Safer Society Press (Bandon, 1993).

Joel Dyer, *The Perpetual Prisoner Machine: How America Profits from Crime.* Westview Press (Boulder, 2000). An analysis of the criminal justice system that raises questions about our profit-driven society.

Michel Foucault, trans. by Alan Sheridan, *Discipline and Punish: The Birth of the Prison,* Pantheon Books (New York, 1977). Thorough, scholarly exploration of the origin of prisons and the history of penal theory in the Euro-American world.

Bernie Glassman, *Bearing Witness.* Bell Tower (1998). Contains chapter detailing Fleet Maull's prison experience and transformation.

Chester Himes, *Yesterday Will Make You Cry,* Norton & Company (New York, 1998). A fictionalized account of this crime novelist's own prison time. The original 1950s version was cut and censored by the editor. It has now been reissued in Hines' original version. This new edition is grittier, more honest and poetic.

Bo Lozoff, *We're All Doing Time,* Human Kindness Foundation (Durham, 1985). Bo Lozoff is the pioneer in interfaith prison spiritual work, and the Prison Ashram Project makes this book available free to inmates. Bo's book is probably already in circulation in whatever prison you work with.

Dannie Martin & Peter Sussman. *Committing Journalism: The Prison Writings of Red Hog.* W.W. Norton & Co. (1993). First rate description of life behind bars.

Jarvis Jay Masters, *Finding Freedom: Writings from Death Row*, Padma Publishing (Junction City, 1997). Buddhist prisoner's story of practice inside.

Sister Helen Prejean, *Dead Man Walking*, Random House (New York, 1994). If you've seen the movie, don't skip the book. There is much more material in the book on the death penalty and on pastoral counseling in prison settings.

Christopher Queen, editor, *Engaged Buddhism in the West,* Wisdom Publications (Boston, 2000). See especially, "The Angulimala Lineage: Buddhist Prison Ministries," by Virginia Cohn Parkum and J. Anthony Stultz, p.347.

Wilbert Rideau & Ron Wikberg, *Life Sentences: Rage and Survival Behind Bars*, Time Books (New York, 1992).

John Snelling, *A Buddhist Handbook*, Inner Traditions (Rochester, 1991). An excellent reference.

Wayne S. Wooden and Jay Parke, *Men Behind Bars: Sexual Exploitation in Prison,* Plenum Press (New York, 1982).

Howard Zehr, *Doing Life: Reflections of Men and Women Serving Life Sentences*, Good Books (Philadephia, 1996). Excellent orientation to the unique world of those serving life—a population that needs to be understood by anyone working in institutions with lifers.

Prison Dharma Network has a bookstore on it's website selling these and many other books. www.PrisonDharmaNetwork.org

Resources

For an up-to-date directory of prisoner resources, Buddhist and otherwise, write Prison Dharma Network to request their *Resource Guide for Buddhist Prisoners & Prison Dharma Volunteers*. The guide is free for those who cannot afford it. A donation is requested from those who can. PDN also has many resource for volunteers on their website.

Prison Dharma Network
P.O. Box 4623
Boulder, CO 80302
www.PrisonDharmaNetwork.org
pdn@indra.com

Prison Dharma Network

is a nonsectarian Buddhist support network for prisoners, prison volunteers and correctional staff. Our mission is to make the dharma and practice of meditation readily available to those wishing to transform their lives and the lives of others within our prisons and jails.

Our ability to distribute this book free-of-charge to prisoners depends on your donations. Please help us put this wonderful manual for self-transformation in the hands of as many prisoners as possible.

Please send your donation to:
Prison Dharma Network
PO Box 4623
Boulder CO 80306

Index

216